DATE DUE			

THE ROLE OF SCIENCE AND TECHNOLOGY
IN DEVELOPING COUNTRIES

The Role of Science and Technology in Developing Countries

GRAHAM JONES

With an Introduction by Professor Lord Blackett

Published for

The International Council of Scientific Unions

by

OXFORD UNIVERSITY PRESS

LONDON   NEW YORK   TORONTO

1971

Oxford University Press, Ely House, London W.1

GLASGOW NEW YORK TORONTO MELBOURNE WELLINGTON
CAPE TOWN SALISBURY IBADAN NAIROBI DAR ES SALAAM LUSAKA ADDIS ABABA
BOMBAY CALCUTTA MADRAS KARACHI LAHORE DACCA
KUALA LUMPUR SINGAPORE HONG KONG TOKYO

Clothbound edition SBN 19 215942 9
Paperbound edition SBN 19 215943 7

309.2232
J7/r
79707
Sept. 1972

Printed in Great Britain
by Ebenezer Baylis & Son Limited
The Trinity Press, Worcester, and London

Contents

Introduction

by LORD BLACKETT

The object of this book is to explore the ways by which modern science and technology can help to promote economic and social growth in the poor but developing countries. The urgency of this task is related to the widening gap between the rich and the poor. Unless great efforts are made the gap will be still wider—and disastrously wider—by the end of the century.

The immediate origin of the book lay in 1966 at the General Assembly of the International Council of Scientific Unions (ICSU). This took place under the chairmanship of Professor H. W. Thompson, Foreign Secretary of the Royal Society, in the Tata Institute of Fundamental Research in Bombay.

Towards the end of a week of meetings and discussions, several delegates expressed the view that ICSU should attempt to do more to help the less developed countries of the world. It was pointed out that the traditional activities of ICSU were mainly concerned with the organizational needs of the basic sciences in an international setting, and that it fulfilled this role very well. Naturally, therefore, ICSU had been more concerned with the advancement of science for its own sake, rather than with the use of science for the practical purpose of improving the welfare of mankind. Perhaps part of the motivation of these speakers may have been influenced by the contrast between the high standard of life of the countries from which many of those attending the General Assembly came and the deep poverty of the majority of the inhabitants of the less developed countries of the world—so much in evidence, for instance, in parts of the great city of Bombay.

Of course, over periods of decades the advancement of basic scientific knowledge provides the possibility of greatly improved living standards for mankind. But scientists are becoming increasingly aware that the application of new scientific knowledge to increase human welfare is a long and expensive matter—often much longer and more expensive in manpower and money than the acquirement of the new knowledge itself.

The suggestion made at the meeting was essentially that ICSU should engage in some activity which would encourage the application of scientific knowledge to increase the well-being of the poor but developing countries. After much discussion the Assembly brought into being a new body with the title 'Committee on Science and Technology in Developing Countries'—COSTED. The members were drawn from twelve countries with myself as chairman.

It was clear from the outset that COSTED could not hope to acquire big enough financial resources to play an important direct role as a provider of money or technological aid to the developing countries. This is evident when one remembers that the total financial aid from the developed countries (DCs) to the less developed countries (LDCs) is around thirteen billion dollars a year, or four per cent of the Gross National Product (GNP) of the LDCs. Of this sum perhaps a hundred million dollars or so a year is spent on scientific research and technological development.

Since, therefore, COSTED could not possibly enter the league of big donors of aid, it had to seek some other distinctive role, if it were to justify bringing together once or twice a year a group of senior and busy scientists. After much discussion COSTED concluded that it might do a valuable service if it made a detailed study of how science and technology can lead to the economic and social betterment of the LDCs. Paraphrasing Rutherford's famous dictum, one could say that 'Since COSTED has no money, it must think'.

Accepting, then, an intellectual role for COSTED, it was decided that a small book with the title *The Role of Science and Technology in Developing Countries* should be produced which would be intended to be of use to scientists and technologists who work in less developed countries or are otherwise interested in their problems. At the same time the book could be offered in a more tentative manner to people in positions of responsibility both in the LDCs and also to those in DCs who are concerned with the Aid and Development Programmes.

In its treatment of the role of science, the book is intended to be primarily concerned with its role in economic development rather than with the broader and more philosophic viewpoint in which science is seen as an important element in culture and learning.

In no sense does the book try to impose a pattern of development which would wipe out social, political, and cultural differences between nations. Rather it is intended to help a developing nation to achieve whatever goals it sets itself. Development is and must be a major national responsibility. But the rest of the world should and must help to the maximum of its capacity. To help the LDCs their problems must be understood. This book is meant to contribute to this understanding.

The arrangements made by COSTED to get such a book written were as follows. The finance to engage an author full time for two years to work under my general direction was shared between ICSU and the Royal Society, and I was to write an introduction explaining the origin of the book.

After discussions with the Overseas Development Institute, the terms of reference were drafted and agreed, and Mr. Graham Jones was appointed by the Institute as the Research Officer responsible for the study. His experience suited him well for this task, as it combined initial training as a chemist, with subsequently many years of scientific and technical administration in several LDCs, in three continents. At the General Assembly of ICSU at Madrid in September 1970, the outline of the book and the plans for publication were approved.

The content of the book was planned taking fully into account the large literature already existing on the problems of the developing countries. This literature covers a very wide range of subject and form, from wide global surveys to highly detailed studies. However, many of these studies are hard to come by and only a small fraction of them could be studied in detail by a working qualified scientist or engineer (QSE), if only for lack of time. The book therefore contains an extensive bibliography and many of the previous studies are critically evaluated in the text. One reason why it was thought that such a book would be timely is that in recent years important advances in understanding have been made, both in the DCs and in the LDCs, of just how the process of innovation takes place—meaning by the word 'innovation' the whole process from scientific discovery or invention to the final emergence of a marketable product, or a social service.

It was not to be expected that the book would contain any novel insights—rather its main aim is to use this extensive literature to help to create a climate of opinion realistically favourable to economic and social development. In effect the book is intended as an educational guide-book to a complex scene rather than a work of new learning. Clearly any such book will be controversial: for the issues are highly complex and there may be many different views which can be legitimately held on many aspects of the problems. It is therefore not to be expected that every member of COSTED, nor of the General Assembly of ICSU, will agree with all the contents of the book. Other views might be expressed in possible future publications of COSTED.

Perhaps the most influential of former studies of many of these problems is the Lester Pearson Report, *Partners in Development*. Its main emphasis is on the economic and social development of the LDCs and on the vital role of financial and technical aid from the DCs. Some wise things are said on the role of science and technology but the treatment does not go into much detail and in some respects may need modification. In a sense this book provides some extra chapters to the Pearson Report, dealing with the role of science and technology in much greater detail.

To get science and technology used to best advantage for the benefit of the LDCs it is not sufficient that a few top economic and social planners should understand what should be done: this must also be understood in the research laboratory, at the industrial work bench and in the fields. Thus a somewhat flippant and even presumptuous sub-title of this book might be 'What Every QSE Ought to Know'.

It is necessary to point out that the material on which the book is based, both facts and theories, is taken mainly from the 'western' countries operating some form of market economy. Unfortunately, relevant studies from the planned economies of Eastern Europe and the People's Republic of China are less often available, though some of the few that have come to our notice are highly pertinent. It may be noted that the existence of such a wealth of literature from western sources is not unconnected with the large aid programmes from the western DCs to the LDCs in four continents. The study of the actual processes of aid in an LDC often leads to important new insights into the micro-processes of economic growth. Since western aid seems at present to be greater in volume than eastern aid, more of these lessons are of western origin.

The book does not attempt to deal specifically with those important and complex problems which LDCs must face in connection with public health and medicine. A good general standard of health is important for economic development. Indeed, the present levels of development in most LDCs would have been impossible without the substantial achievements which, backed by much excellent scientific research, have been to the credit of the medical and public health services; one result of these efforts is dramatically seen in the rapid growth of population which has been such a feature of the last few decades. Much remains to be done to maintain and improve health standards, but for most LDCs it is perhaps still more important to establish or expand effective family planning services on a large scale. No one questions the overriding importance on a world scale of achieving a drastic drop in population growth, e.g. from 2·5 to 1·5 per cent per annum. But the subject has been studied so often and so well that it will not be discussed at all in this book.

Another aspect which is only touched on relates to the image of science in the world as a whole and in the LDCs in particular. Today there are undoubtedly signs of reaction against science, or perhaps more accurately against some of the claims of science. In my youth, over fifty years ago, science was pursued on such a small scale that it did not notably impinge on the mass of the population, nor for that matter on governments. Then came a great quickening of the pace of science, partly due to the two world wars, and a vast increase in its expense. These tendencies were heightened by the advent of nuclear energy and space exploration, etc., and in the biological field by antibiotics, etc. The power of science seemed to some without limit. In the United Kingdom and the United States in the early 1960s, science budgets rose by up to 15 per cent a year, many times higher than the growth rates of GNPs. Science had arrived and seemed to sweep all before it.

A reaction to this overselling of science was bound to come. Rates of rise of expenditure on science began to be cut: in some countries big absolute cuts have been made in certain fields. Scientists had to stand up and justify themselves and their actions and demands on society. Except perhaps for a core of high-class basic research, scientific research and development is increasingly matched against promised economic and social gains: that is, in the present jargon, with its 'relevance' to social needs.

Just because the role of science and technology in the DCs is now being critically examined, it has become of vital importance that its role in LDCs be really well clarified. Though mainly the job of the LDCs themselves, the DCs can and must help, drawing on their successes and failures in managing technologically advanced economies. Then, of course, much of the science and technology in the LDCs is or can be greatly helped through the aid programme from the DCs. If scientific and technical aid is to be fruitful, then it is important to understand the mechanism by which research and development can raise the rate of economic growth in the recipient countries. It is equally important to understand what science cannot do as well as what it can.

Unless the internal resources spent by an LDC on research and development are wisely used, the country can be made poorer, not richer. Moreover, the reaction against science and modern technology may grow and could prove very damaging to the future of an LDC.

Since the book is about what technology and science can do to assist the economic growth of the LDCs, it would be fitting to finish my introduction by outlining the present economic situation of the LDCs and the DCs.

In the Organization of Economic Co-operation and Development (OECD) classification, there are 15 main rich donor countries and 28 main poor less developed countries. The former have a population of 600 million with a GNP of $2,500 per head. The latter have a population of 1,600 million and a GNP a head of $150, that is 1/17 of that of the former, say in round figures, 1/20. These average figures cover wide ranges. For instance, a few years ago the *per capita* incomes of the United States and of India were $3,500 and $90 respectively, giving a ratio of 40 to 1. This ratio is still increasing. The total GNP of the donor countries is six times that of the recipient countries.

Since the net rate of rise of the GNP a head of the rich countries is 3·5 per cent compared with 2·5 per cent for the poor countries, the rich countries are getting richer 1 per cent faster than the poor countries. So the gap is still widening. If present trends continue until A.D. 2000, then the arithmetic excess of the GNP a head of the rich countries over that of the poor will have risen from about $2,500 to $7,000. Another way of looking at the gap is to note that the annual added wealth of a citizen of a rich country is nearly as much as a citizen of a poor country has to live on for a whole year.

If the relative gap is to be halved, say, from the present 20 to 1 to 10 to 1, by A.D. 2000, i.e. in 30 years, then the net rate of increase of GNP of the LDCs will have to be raised from the present 1 per cent below to 2 per cent above that of the DCs. The part that generous aid from the rich donor countries to the poor recipient countries could play in bringing this about is very fully discussed in the Lester Pearson Report. If such an increased growth rate of the LDCs is to be attained, very large resources will have to be invested, mainly from internal resources, but one hopes also from aid from the DCs.

The degree to which modern science and technology can assist this growth process will depend on the total amount of investment funds available, the fraction allocated by the government of any country to science and technology (in competition with all the other social demands), and the wisdom and skill with which these financial resources are used.

Nov. 1970

The Committee on Science and Technology in
Developing Countries (COSTED) of the
International Council of Scientific Unions (ICSU)

MEMBERSHIP (on 21 July 1970):
  Professor Lord Blackett (U.K.)   (Chairman)
  Professor Harrison Brown (U.S.A.)
  Professor W. K. Chagula (Tanzania)
  Professor K. Chandrasekharan (India)
  Professor V. Deulofeu (Argentina)
  Dr. J. M. Harrison (Canada)
  Professor A. K. Katchalsky (Israel)
  Academician Ya. V. Peyve (U.S.S.R.)
  Professor S. Prawirohardjo (Indonesia)
  Professor M. Roy (France)

SECRETARY:
  Mr. F. W. G. Baker (ICSU Secretariat)

PREVIOUS MEMBERS:
  Professor R. V. Garcia (Argentina)
  Professor M. Ishidate (Japan)
  Professor I. Malecki (Poland)
  Professor F. Seitz (U.S.A.)

Acknowledgements

My greatest debt is to the three organizations—to ICSU, and especially its committee COSTED, to the Royal Society, and to the Overseas Development Institute—which made it possible for me to write this book. How it came to be written has been described by Lord Blackett in the Introduction. I should like to record here the special pleasure it has been to work in close collaboration with someone of such perception and understanding as Lord Blackett. I must thank also the individual members of COSTED, who have given me many useful suggestions, and I want to acknowledge especially the help and encouragement I have received from Professor K. Chandrasekharan, at that time Secretary-General of ICSU, as well as a member of COSTED. The staff of the Royal Society have been most helpful, but I am particularly indebted to Dr. R. W. J. Keay, the Deputy Executive Secretary, who has been a constant source of valuable comments and suggestions. The Overseas Development Institute, too, provided strong support throughout the study in the form of expert advice from its staff, and the use of its library facilities.

In preparing this book, extensive use has been made of a very diverse range of published material, which has been collected mainly through the generous help of a large number of individuals and institutions throughout the world. In addition, many people have taken a great deal of trouble to write at length on various aspects of the subject matter of this book. It is not possible here to mention them all by name, but I gratefully acknowledge the important contribution which they have made.

Many people, too, were kind enough to read the first draft, and to offer a great number of suggestions for improvement. In particular I should like to thank Professor A. H. Bunting of Reading University; Mr. Guy Gresford, United Nations Director of Science and Technology; Sir Arthur Gaitskell, Director of the Commonwealth Development Corporation;

Sir Eric Ashby, Master of Clare College, Cambridge; Sir Joseph Hutchinson, Emeritus Professor of Agriculture, Cambridge; Mr. D. G. Chisman of the Centre for Educational Development Overseas; and the staff of the Overseas Development Institute, specially Dr. T. Soper, Professor Guy Hunter, and Mr. Bruce Dinwiddy.

Finally I should like to express my appreciation of the kindness of R.T.Z. Consultants Ltd. in allowing my secondment to the Overseas Development Institute for the period of this study.

In acknowledging the generous help I have received from so many people, I do not of course imply any responsibility on their part for the views expressed or for the accuracy of the text.

GRAHAM JONES

I Science and Technology in Economic Development

THE LESS-DEVELOPED WORLD

One aspect of one of the world's most serious problems is strikingly summarized in a simple chart presented in the Report of the Pearson Commission:[1]

FIGURE I

Source: Report of the Pearson Commission, p. 24.

About two thirds of the world's population have average annual earnings of only $135 per head, while the remainder in the developed countries enjoy $1,800 per head.

Over the period 1950–67, the less developed countries succeeded in increasing their Gross Domestic Product[2] at an average annual rate of 4·8 per cent. But over the same period their population increased at 2·4 per cent per annum, reducing the average GDP increase per head to 2·4 per cent per annum. Though economic growth was rather less rapid in the industrialized countries, their populations were more stable, so that GDP per head showed a net increase of 3·1 per cent per

[1] Lester B. Pearson: *Partners in Development.* Report of the Commission on International Development, London, 1969.
[2] Gross Domestic Product (GDP) measures the value of all the goods and services produced within the country during a year. Gross National Product (GNP) equals Gross Domestic Product minus net income payments abroad such as income on foreign investment. (Report of Pearson Commission.)

annum. These rates of growth signify relatively little without taking into account the respective bases to which they apply. The GDP of a rich country may *increase* in two years by $120 per head, which is more than the total GDP per head in many countries, such as India or Indonesia.

Thus the rich industrialized countries, already far ahead, are drawing still further away from the less developed countries, worsening a dangerously explosive situation. For not only are the people of the poorer nations aware that these differences exist and are growing, but they are generally felt to be due, in part at least, to past and present exploitation.

The overall figures which have been cited cover an enormous range of variation between individual countries, which makes a rigorous definition of a developing country almost impossible. While a country with average annual earnings of less than $600 would generally be accepted as a developing country, there are many borderline cases. As the Pearson Report has emphasized, though most of the countries in Asia, Africa, and Latin America are separated from the developed countries by a wide economic gulf, whether one considers income per head, social conditions, demographic characteristics, or the structure of production, 'any nomenclature inevitably does violence to the overwhelming diversity which the developing countries present'.

Two elements of this diversity are shown in Table 1, which stratifies countries by population and GNP per head. Superimposed on these are a wide range of population densities, natural resource endowments, social, political, and economic systems, and historical backgrounds. Though on average almost equally impoverished, the problems of a small land-locked country like Chad, with few highly trained nationals and severely limited resources, are evidently very different from those of large countries like India, with a widely-based education system of relatively long standing and substantial industrial development. Even within a country the diversity may be enormous, with vast differences between classes or between regions. In Brazil, for example, State Domestic Income ranged from $750 per head in the province around Rio to about $75 per head in part of the north-east. In respect of development, each country, and often each region within a country, must be regarded as a special case.

TABLE I

GNP (US$) per capita vs *Population × 1 million (m.)*

GNP (US$) per capita	1–2·5	2·6–5·0	5·1–10·0	10·1–20·0	20·1–50·0	50·1++	
0–50		Somalia, Burundi 6m.	Upper Volta 5m.				11m.
51–100	Togo, Dahomey 4m.	Mali, Malawi, Laos, Haiti, Chad, Niger, Rwanda, Guinea 30m.	Yemen, Malagasy Rep., Uganda 20m.	Afghanistan, Nepal, Tanzania, Sudan, Congo (K) 69m.	Ethiopia, Burma, N. Vietnam 70m.	Nigeria, Pakistan, India, Indonesia, China 1523m.	1716m.
101–150	Mauritania, Cent. Afri. Rep., Sierra Leone, S. Yemen 6m.		Cameroon, Cambodia, Kenya 22m.	Rep. Vietnam 20m.	Thailand 33m.		81m.
151–200	Papua & N. Guinea, Liberia 3m.	Bolivia, Zambia, Senegal 11m.	Angola, Syria, Mozambique, Ghana 26m.	Ceylon, Morocco 26m.	R. of Korea, U.A.R., Philippines 95m.		161m.
201–300	Paraguay, Jordan, Honduras 7m.	S. Rhodesia, El Salvador, Ivory Coast, Dominican Rep., Tunisia 25m.	Ecuador, Iraq 14m.	Algeria, Taiwan, Colombia, Malaysia, N. Korea 66m.	Iran, Turkey 59m.	Brazil 86m.	257m.
301–400	Albania, Nicaragua 4m.	Guatemala 5m.	Saudi Arabia, Cuba 15m.	Peru 12m.			36m.
401–500	Costa Rica, Jamaica, Mongolia 5m.		Portugal, Chile 19m.		Mexico 46m.		70m.
501–600	Singapore, Panama 3m.	Uruguay 3m.		Yugoslavia, S. Africa 39m.			45m.
601–700	Lebanon 3m.	Hong Kong 4m.	Bulgaria, Greece 17m.		Spain 32m.		56m.
	35m.	84m.	138m.	232m.	335m.	1609m.	2433m.

Source: Based on World Bank data for 1967.

This book is concerned with the application of science and technology to economic growth in less developed countries (LDCs). This problem has become more acute in recent decades, when dozens of sovereign countries have appeared on the world stage. Peoples of these countries are faced with a choice of ways for economic development, while real opportunities have opened up for such a choice. Development, of course, involves far more than material growth, and there may be many views about ultimate goals. Few today are likely to hold that any increase in material wealth, even if equitably distributed, will necessarily bring a corresponding increase in human happiness and personal fulfilment, but few will deny the importance of alleviating extreme poverty. As Galbraith has said recently 'The test of social achievement is not the annual increase in output of a society but how well the society addresses itself to the tacks which improve the lives of its members.'[1] However, countries with lower living standards do need a higher rate of economic growth.

Economic and social change in the LDCs must depend primarily on the actions of these countries themselves, their peoples and their governments. The successful achievement of the conditions necessary for speedy economic development is possible only if this is accepted as a priority objective, and if governments pursue stable policies directed towards this end, using modern methods and forms of management and administration of national economies. In other words, science and technology alone can make little contribution without the will to advance economically, and the opportunity and organization to use them. 'Unless the social and political structure of the country is such as to put economic growth on high priority, neither education, nor management skills, nor capital, nor science and technology, nor all together, will raise the living standards of the mass of the population.'[2]

But the world economy in which this development must take place is largely dominated by the highly industrialized countries, and tends to favour the rich at the expense of the poor. The

[1] From an article by Professor J. K. Galbraith published in Japan, and reported in the London *Times*, 2 September 1970.

[2] Lord Blackett: *Reflexions on science and technology in developing countries*. Gandhi Memorial Lectures, East African Publishing House, Nairobi, January 1969. No. I, p. 14.

application of science and technology in the developed countries, particularly through the development of synthetics and advanced science-based industries, makes economic advance in LDCs increasingly difficult, and almost impossible without the co-operation of the developed countries. The efforts of the LDCs must be supplemented and supported by the developed countries, through financial and technical assistance and multilateral co-operative arrangements. Such co-operation is in line with the vital interests of all technologically developed nations. Reducing the economic gap between developed and developing countries, through a faster rate of growth among the poorer nations, must be a priority concern of the entire world.

ECONOMIC GROWTH AND TECHNICAL PROGRESS

The material wealth of a country depends on the production of goods and services through the co-ordinated use of the available supplies of human skills, capital, land, and natural resources. Economic growth can stem from greater production through the use of more resources, and from greater productivity through the more efficient use of resources. Technology contributes to both aspects, through increasing the utility of available resources—as for example in allowing the productive use of land previously considered infertile, or by discovering an economic use for a raw material previously thought valueless— and by productivity improvements through increased skills, better methods, and better machines. Science provides the pool of basic knowledge and understanding on which technology increasingly depends.

It is important to distinguish between science and technology. In brief, technology is 'know-how' while science is 'know-why'. Science produces knowledge, technology helps to produce wealth.[1] Historically, science has been more dependent on technology than vice versa, and only recently have science-based industries come to the fore. Even now they must be regarded as mainly separate streams, with a limited though increasing interaction. In either, growth tends to depend on the state of the art of each separately, with old technology breeding new technology and old science breeding new science.

[1] Atma Ram: 'Science—our new responsibility'. Anniversary address, National Institute of Sciences of India, 2 January 1970.

Many technological advances involve no new scientific principles, though the nature of scientific development may have a long-term influence on the kinds of technological change which may be feasible. A specific scientific discovery may take many years before it finds practical application. A recent investigation prepared for the U.S. National Science Foundation entitled *TRACES (Technology in Retrospect and Critical Events in Science)*[1] attempts to trace historically the key scientific events which led towards five major technological innovations. Non-mission or basic research 'provided the origins from which science and technology could advance towards the innovations which lay ahead', but particularly work done between 20 and 30 years before the innovation.

According to the science historian, de Solla Price, 'the naive picture of technology as applied science simply will not fit all the facts'.[2] There is, however, a symbiotic relationship between them—'science without the byplay of technology becomes sterile' while technology without science becomes moribund.

But science is available in a world-wide system of publications, accessible to anyone who knows the language. Technology is not so readily accessible, partly because of industrial secrecy and property rights, but also because technology must be learnt by doing. It is embodied experience, and is inherently much more difficult to transfer, though in one way or another a large amount of modern technology and know-how does in fact get transferred. In the development of biological natural resources, technology is essentially dependent on the environment, and hence must be devised to suit each ecological situation.

Investment of resources in science and technology can bring substantial economic returns, as can investment in education and training. Yet they must not be regarded as isolated activities deserving of some support, but as components of a dynamic system to convert human skills and enterprise into new material wealth and social amenities. The effective use of the achievements of science and technology requires the removal of all obstacles of a political, social, and economic character, which

---

[1] *Technology in Retrospect and Critical Events in Science*, 1968.

[2] D. J. de Solla Price: 'The structures of publication in science and technology'. In *Factors in the Transfer of Technology*, ed. by W. H. Gruber and D. G. Marquis, MIT Press, 1969, p. 91.

have been inherited by LDCs from the past stages of their history. Science and technology constitute but one factor of change, which must be integrated into the overall economic and social development plan.

In most developing countries, lack of scientific and technological knowledge is seldom a critical limiting factor—the main obstacles to application are economic and social, including education, communications, acceptability of new ideas, administrative effectiveness, business enterprise, and political leadership. Social and cultural traditions are often positive barriers to change, and economic growth will require extensive and intensive changes in human values and attitudes, as well as in social and political structures. Only within this broader context of development, can science and technology make an effective contribution.

INDUSTRIALIZED COUNTRIES

In view of the success which industrialized countries have had in applying science and technology to economic development, though not without considerable social costs, it seems reasonable to study this experience to see what lessons can be learned which may be of value to developing nations, not only in relation to the more modern science-based industries, but also in the broader process of industrialization and productivity improvement.

Traditional economic theories are of limited use in an analysis of the economic effects of technological change, but it is now generally accepted that much if not most of the economic growth of industrialized countries may be attributed to technical progress, taken to include better organization and management, more skilful and effective labour, as well as improved materials, processes, and equipment.[1] The benefits of technical change are achieved at the cost of heavy investments in education and training, in research and development (R and D), and in capital equipment embodying the results of R and D. Such heavy investment implies a temporary reduction in the living standards of the people.

[1] B. R. Williams: *Technology, Investment and Growth*. Chapman & Hall, London, 1967, p. 67.

New knowledge by itself makes no contribution to economic growth, nor does an invention generated by scientific or technical advances. Only when the knowledge or the invention is incorporated effectively into the production system can economic growth result. One of the key factors in growth is innovation, the culminating stage of the total scientific and technological effort. In market economy terms, this may be defined as the commercial exploitation of technical knowledge to win new markets, or hold existing ones against competition, by reducing costs of production of conventional goods or introducing novel or more efficient goods.[1] Similarly, according to the terminology of the planned economy, innovation involves the intentional introduction of the achievements of science and technology into production to cut down production costs, to improve labour conditions and to speed up the general rate of economic growth, to meet the growing needs of the population.

The stocks of technical knowledge on which innovation depends can be increased by R and D. But it must be recognized that R and D is only part of the total innovation process, and is not in itself a cause of economic growth. Economically speaking R and D expenditure is in fact simply an overhead expense until the results are commercially exploited through innovation. R and D is but the first stage in the process, and the importance is now recognized of a continuous innovative chain linking scientific research, marketing research, invention, development design, tooling, first production, and marketing of the new product.[2] R and D usually involves a relatively small proportion of the total cost of a successful innovation, as indicated in Figure 2, and in budgeting for innovation the entire cost, not only R and D, must be anticipated. Within the R and D component itself the development stages will account for a much greater part of this expenditure than scientific research, which thus becomes a relatively small part of the total innovation costs.

In market economies, innovation and investment are closely

---

[1] Central Advisory Council for Science and Technology: *Technological Innovation in Britain*. HMSO, 1968, p. 1.

[2] R. A. Charpie: *Technological Innovation—Its Environment and Management*. U.S. Dept. of Commerce, 1967, p. 8.

tied, for not only does a potentially profitable innovation stimulate investment, but a high level of investment tends to encourage innovation, to take advantage of the latest technological advances. In general, the major drive towards successful innovation stems from the market, whether an existent or a potential demand.

Essentially then, R and D is a response to pressures from the marketing function, through the production function, for new or improved products or processes, or reduced production costs. Even within a single organization the application of R and D results is not a spontaneous operation, but requires a directed and planned effort. The greater the separation of R and D from production, the more difficult does the coupling become, with increasing risks of R and D being undertaken which is irrelevant to production or market needs, or conversely of production problems left unresolved.

These difficulties have arisen in planned industrial economies, as well as in free enterprise economies. In East Germany, for example, where research is carried out in centralized institutes, the system has been re-organized during recent years so that

FIGURE 2
TYPICAL DISTRIBUTION OF COSTS IN SUCCESSFUL PRODUCT INNOVATIONS

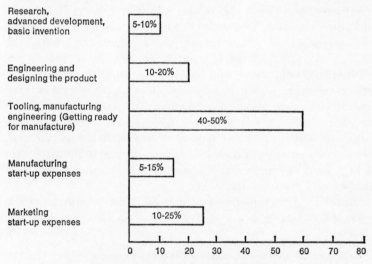

Source: Charpie, *Technological Innovation.*

now, apart from special arrangements for 'discovery research', no research work is undertaken except on the specific request of a social body.[1]

Whatever the economic system, the innovation process can be upset at any stage and may be affected by a wide range of factors. If R and D does not lead to innovation because other factors are not favourable, such as an inadequate market, the expenditure may be largely wasted.

The relationship between R and D expenditure and national economics is complex, and several countries have spent a great deal of money on R and D in recent years, without achieving spectacular economic growth, as indicated in Figure 3. While the U.S. and the U.K. were high research spenders during the 1950s, their subsequent growth rates have been comparatively poor. On the other hand, at that time Japan and West Germany spent relatively much less on R and D, but had higher growth rates.

In part this apparent lack of correlation may be related to the fact that R and D is but a part of the innovative process. 'But in this area it is extremely difficult to distinguish between cause and effect: is it innovation which causes growth, or growth which causes innovation?'[2]

It must of course be recognized that both Japan and West Germany had been first-class scientific powers for many decades and hence were able to make good use of technological developments in other countries. Furthermore, with the exception of Japan and West Germany, most highly industrialized countries spend considerable sums on military and space research, which have uncertain spin-off effects in civil industry. In most Western countries about 50 per cent of R and D expenditure is not oriented to economic growth. But in addition, while Japan and West Germany spent less on research, they allocated more of their GNP to investment in industry, and a high level of investment is a prerequisite to ensure growth of output and productivity.

Another important factor which must be considered is the

[1] H. Kautzleben: 'Tasks and Aims of the Academy Reform in the German Democratic Republic'. Paper presented at the International Symposium on the Relations between Science and Technology, Bratislava, 1969.

[2] *The role of the government in research and development.* Occasional Paper No. 4, Hill Samuel & Co. Ltd., London, 1969, p. 9.

availability of qualified manpower. The application of new technical knowledge to production and manufacture requires trained personnel at all stages of the innovation process, capable of identifying needs and solving problems. In practice, innovation may arise not only from R and D, but from operational improvements by managerial or production personnel. A large number of minor improvements introduced by productivity-conscious staff may be more important than a small number of dramatic innovations. This is particularly evidenced in the mechanical engineering field, as for example in the case of the motor-car.

FIGURE 3

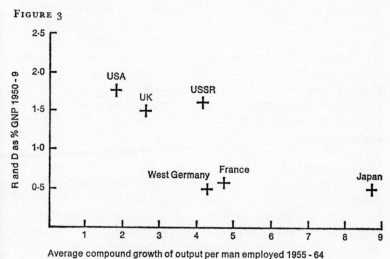

Source: Williams, *Technology, Investment and Growth.*

Qualified technical and managerial personnel are needed throughout industry, and are invariably in short supply. The distribution of this staff between the various stages of the innovation chain is critical in the optimum deployment of such limited resources. Williams[1] has shown that R and D may be excessive, and may actually hinder growth, as for instance where the output is greater than the capacity of industry to absorb. In this case capacity can be increased by a redeployment of scientists and technologists away from R and D into

[1] B. R. Williams: 'Research and Economic Growth: What should we expect?' *Minerva*, III, No. 1, Autumn 1964, p. 65.

production. Such a redeployment of skilled personnel is obviously very difficult, but is being attempted, for example, in the U.K.

Furthermore, it is not necessary, nor normally practicable, to rely entirely on one's own R and D. The results of scientific research are available internationally through publications, and the results of most technological research are available through the market place—in the shape of new machines or materials, or through the purchase of patents and licences. Technical know-how is a standard commodity in international markets.

The international exchange of know-how is shown by the 'technological balance of payments', which compares a country's payments to other countries for technical know-how, licences, and patents, with its receipts for these items. The statistical base is somewhat crude as yet, but estimates for 1964, based on OECD (Organization for Economic Co-operation and Development) data and excluding transactions among socialist countries and between those countries and developing countries, are shown in Figure 4. Even with a relatively high rate of R and D expenditure, the U.K. could hardly produce more than about 10 per cent of the world's technological discoveries, and so had to rely heavily on buying from outside. But the U.K. sold about as much as she bought, while countries such as West Germany, France, and Japan had an adverse technological balance of payments. In the special post-war circumstances, given their high scientific absorptive capacity, this may indicate a wise use of resources, allowing a higher concentration of qualified technical personnel in production and sales. In general, it would seem that any country, even the U.S. and the U.S.S.R., must buy technology from abroad, but to be able to do so most profitably, it needs an internal R and D effort to adapt and absorb. High investment rates are necessary for full use of the latest techniques, even when these are bought abroad, since such techniques are often incorporated in expensive capital equipment.

IMPLICATIONS FOR LESS DEVELOPED COUNTRIES

These experiences in industrialized countries have important implications for less developed countries, where technical and managerial personnel are even more limited, and the production structure does not normally create a spontaneous demand for innovations. In such circumstances technological autarchy is a self-defeating policy, and a satisfactory strategy for technical progress must involve an optimum combination of assimilating scientific and technological advances from other countries, with an indigenous organization for research, development, innovation, and diffusion.

FIGURE 4
TECHNOLOGICAL BALANCE OF PAYMENTS: ESTIMATES FOR 1964

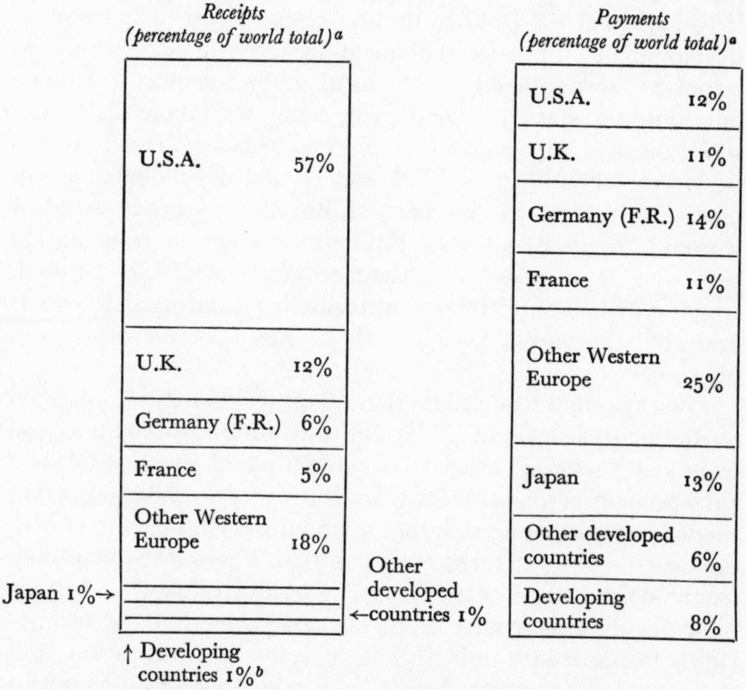

Receipts (percentage of world total)[a]	Payments (percentage of world total)[a]
U.S.A. 57%	U.S.A. 12%
	U.K. 11%
	Germany (F.R.) 14%
	France 11%
U.K. 12%	Other Western Europe 25%
Germany (F.R.) 6%	
France 5%	Japan 13%
Other Western Europe 18%	Other developed countries 6%
Japan 1%→	
Other developed ←countries 1%	Developing countries 8%
↑ Developing countries 1%[b]	

[a] Excluding transactions among socialist countries and between those countries and developing countries.

[b] Receipts of developing countries were negligible and in any case less than 1 per cent.

Source: C. D. G. Oldham, C. Freeman, and E. Turkcan: *Transfer of technology to developing countries.* Study of the Science Policy Research Unit of the University of Sussex, for the U.N. Conference on Trade and Development, Second Session. TD/28/Supp. 1, 10 November 1967. (Based on OECD data)

Innovation and diffusion will require active encouragement and stimulation. In India, it has been said that the biggest obstacle to innovation most often arises from social factors within organizations rather than the absence of technological know-how or equipment.[1] In each country, the socio-economic and political factors inhibiting the effective application of science and technology need to be analysed and practical means for overcoming them devised.

The application of science and technology to economic and social problems should not be considered as synonymous with research. Many problems may be solved using existing knowledge, without the need to do any research. In early stages of development, countries will need to rely almost entirely on imported technologies, with local efforts concentrated on adaptation to suit local conditions, resources, labour skills, and social institutions. As development proceeds local resources can be increasingly allocated to R and D, and dependence on imported technology can be reduced. But at any stage it would be wasteful to apply severely limited resources to re-inventing technologies already in existence and available through copying or licensing. Imported technology and local R and D are not alternative policies, they must complement each other.

The capacity to assimilate and adapt technology will depend on the general level of skills, the distribution of scientific and technical personnel, and the availability of managerial and entrepreneurial talent. Management is one of the most important single factors in modern industry, and has a vital part to play in the creative and efficient use of available resources, including technologists. The experience of industrialized countries indicates the importance of encouraging scientists and technologists to move into industry, agriculture, administration, and management generally, rather than take an exclusive interest in research. Innovative designers and engineers on the workshop floor are likely to prove more useful than space-age scientists. Of particular importance, too, are supporting services—documentation and information centres, natural

---

[1] V. A. Sarabhai: 'Implementing change through science and technology'. Inventory Conference and the International Symposium on Science and Society in South Asia, New York, 1966.

resource surveys, standards institutes, testing and quality control laboratories, management development and productivity centres—all necessary foundations to sound industrial growth, and all requiring scientific and technical personnel.

In appropriate circumstances, imported industrial technology can be assimilated fairly readily, though there may be economic and social advantages from an adaptation to suit the local situation. But in agriculture, though scientific principles remain valid, the package of technology must be designed specifically to match the ecological conditions, in addition to taking account of economic, social, historical, and cultural factors. Adaptive research in this field is therefore essential.

In most developing countries, and indeed in most developed countries, there is a severe shortage of qualified staff to serve all these needs. This situation is likely to continue for some time, as the stock of trained manpower can be increased only relatively slowly and many qualified people are absorbed in the training process. It is vital therefore to ensure that this limiting resource is deployed to best advantage, and that overall requirements and priorities are taken into account in the formulation of education and science policies.

SCIENCE POLICY

Most industrialized countries with market economies have during recent years found it necessary to create instruments at the highest executive level to formulate science and technology policies, and to co-ordinate plans for the most effective use of scientific and technical resources. Certain countries with planned economies have gained considerable experience in the formulation of national policy on the development of science and technology as well as the introduction of their results and achievements in industry. With more limited resources, and with a socio-economic structure tending to inhibit the ready adoption of innovations, such policies have even greater importance in less developed countries. But it must be admitted that the industrialized countries themselves, both market and planned economies, have yet to develop fully satisfactory mechanisms for technology planning, and the integration of technology and economic planning. Developing countries may

3

need to experiment with innovational institutions to suit their particular circumstances.

Science policy is much more than a policy for scientific research, and cannot be treated in isolation. The aim is to set science and technology within the framework of national policies for the structural transformation of agriculture and industry. In this context development plans occupy a key position. The overall development plan and science policy interact in that the application of science and technology, from both indigenous and external sources, should be directed towards national, politically determined objectives, while at the same time science and technology can widen the range of options available to the country.

While science and technology have an important role in development, their effects may not be entirely beneficial, as evidenced by the rising problems of pollution and depletion of the world's natural resources. Science cannot be left as an activity independent of the rest of the society, and attempts must be made to assess the consequences of its use. On a world scale, in fact, present R and D may be detrimental to LDCs, for example through synthetics replacing natural products.

The theory of science for development is itself as yet underdeveloped, and there are few general principles to guide optimum allocations. There can, however, be no doubt concerning the importance of correct decisions, and the subject is discussed in greater depth in Chapter II.

AGRICULTURAL DEVELOPMENT

A common feature of almost all LDCs is the large proportion of their people who depend on agriculture, in its broadest sense, for their livelihood. Taking all LDCs together, the agricultural sector contributed about 30 per cent of total GDP, provided over 40 per cent of total exports of goods and services, and supported directly nearly 70 per cent of the total population.[1]

With the current rapid rate of population growth, even at the most optimistic rate of industrialization, the absolute numbers

[1] *Provisional indicative world plan for agricultural development: Summary and main conclusions*, Food and Agricultural Organization of the United Nations, Rome, 1970.

depending directly on agriculture will inevitably increase. The Food and Agriculture Organization[1] estimates that of the extra one billion people anticipated in LDCs by 1985, some 400 million will be in agriculture. Without positive policies towards employment leading to the creation of additional jobs both in agriculture and in related industries, many of these people will be unable to find productive work, so depressing average income, slowing down economic growth and adding to social problems and discontent. The long-term solution of these problems, of course, also demands positive policies on population growth.

Until recent years, for both social and economic reasons, a somewhat pessimistic view has often been taken of the growth potential of the agricultural sector in LDCs. In the face of the population explosion agriculture could provide neither sufficient food nor productive employment, thus driving increasing numbers into the cities. The industrial sector was regarded as the key to economic growth. But the success of the new wheat and rice varieties, particularly in India and Pakistan, has indicated the feasibility, through a combination of new technology and a simultaneous attack on the socio-economic limiting factors, of achieving growth by a balanced development of agriculture and industry.

The problems of agriculture and industry are deeply interlocked. A dynamic agriculture depends on expanding off-farm markets for its products, but in turn it can provide expanding markets for industrial products—both agricultural inputs such as fertilizers, and consumer goods—and can offer increased employment opportunities. But for this picture to become a reality, the large masses of small farmers must be given a satisfactory income through commercial farming. Quite apart from the political and social dangers of great inequality in the distribution of the benefits from development, poverty in a large mass of the population is a tremendous economic constraint.[2]

Agricultural exports to industrialized countries have made, and will continue to make, a substantial contribution to foreign

[1] Ibid.
[2] Sir A. Gaitskell: 'Some problems of development today'. Talk at the Institute of Development Studies, Sussex, 1970.

exchange earnings. But the growth potential in this trade seems limited, especially without substantial changes in trade policy by the developed countries. Internal and regional commercial marketing of goods and services, with the major emphasis in the short term on agricultural and allied products, seems likely to be the main force for growth. As this develops, the transport, storage, and processing of these products will become increasingly important, offering further opportunities for employment and growth.

It has already been emphasized that the new technology from which these developments will stem must be designed to suit the specific ecological circumstances. But besides improved technology, a greater exploitation of biological natural resources will call for a considerable package of changes. The new cereal varieties are the result of a long-term co-operative research effort, but they would have been of little value without a simultaneous comprehensive development programme, as a result of which fertilizers and water were made available in adequate quantities, prices were sustained, financial assistance was provided to farmers, and storage and distribution facilities extended. With these factors acting in concert, the gains have been dramatic, but maintaining the impetus of this improvement will require not only a continuing research effort in anticipation of the new pest and disease problems which are likely to arise, but also considerable social and economic structural adaptation.

The 'Green Revolution' has so far had little impact in most of Africa or in Latin America, with the exception of Mexico. Though it has been shown that peasant farmers do respond to incentives and that, in the words of Barbara Ward, 'wherever the farmer has the market inducement to produce and sell, he will run up a black market in fertilizer before the planners have time to turn round',[1] in many countries agricultural development is held back by outdated social systems and economic institutions. Improvements cannot be expected without substantial changes, including more equitable land tenure, better markets, material supplies, as well as improved technology and strengthened extension services.

[1] Barbara Ward: 'Technological Change and the World Market'. *Applied Science and World Economy*, U.S. House of Representatives, 1968.

Even given the acceptability of social and economic changes, it must be remembered that farming involves a highly-interdependent complex of operations and any new technique is likely to have far-reaching effects. While a great deal is already known about increasing the yields of individual crops, in most tropical areas relatively little is known about the combinations of crops and animals which give the most effective farming systems. Science and technology can make a useful contribution only within a broad systems approach, including mechanisms for introducing the new techniques to the farmers and also for dealing with all the other factors affected. Only in this context can the results of research bring economic returns.

Agricultural research and development, and equally fisheries or forestry research, can be a worthwhile investment, but only if part of a broad integrated development effort. This has important implications for the organization of agricultural research, which are pursued in Chapter III.

INDUSTRIAL DEVELOPMENT

As a country develops, so the role of manufacturing industry in the economy increases. While the availability of capital, skills, and markets limits the rate of industrialization, agriculture must absorb a substantial share of the total manpower, particularly as efficient modern industries often involve high investments in relation to the number of jobs created. But in the long term improved living standards depend on greater labour productivity, and as agriculture becomes more efficient, productive employment will increasingly have to be provided within manufacturing industry. Industrial development and urbanization seems an inevitable process, requiring extensive developments in transportation, communications and construction, for which careful technological planning and innovation will be essential.

From a technical viewpoint, industrial development is more complicated than agriculture, in that manufacturing involves a much wider range of techniques, and there is less incentive in most LDCs to introduce innovations and to adapt known technology to local conditions. While agricultural technology must necessarily be adapted to the specific environment, industrial techniques can usually be transplanted without major modification, however inappropriate they may be. Local entrepreneurs normally show little interest in adapting and improving foreign technology, partly from cultural and social practice, partly from the nature of the production structure, and often from national economic and fiscal policies. For rapid development technological innovation needs positive encouragement.

In many countries manufacturing firms operate behind heavy customs protection, based on import-substitution policies, and so escape the pressures of competition. This situation encourages the use of inefficient technologies and provides little incentive for improvement. Manufacturers then are just not interested in R and D results. Increasingly, however, developing countries are turning attention towards exports, and the requirements of international competitiveness will bring a growing demand for improved know-how.

Typically, the industrial structure of an LDC includes subsidiaries of foreign-owned international corporations; large locally-owned companies, often family businesses, relying mainly on imported know-how; and small local businesses with very limited managerial and technical competence.

The role of foreign corporations and their subsidiaries operating in LDCs is discussed more fully in Chapter IV. They are evidently an effective mechanism for transferring technology, but may involve some loss of local authority, and the very fact that know-how is readily available from the parent tends to preclude any local R and D efforts. However, the terms on which foreign capital investment is permitted do allow governments a significant measure of control and direction. As the Pearson Report says, rather than insisting on the inclusion of domestic investors in foreign subsidiaries, 'it seems better to press for things which give a greater assurance of gain, such as technical and managerial training of local personnel, assistance to local supplying industries, the establishment of a plant large enough to serve export markets, and limited tariff protection and tax concessions'.[1]

Both national and international firms can be encouraged by local fiscal and tax policies to take more interest in adapting imported technologies to suit local needs, and to engage in

[1] Pearson Commission Report, op. cit., p. 112.

relevant R and D. There seems scope for greater assistance from international agencies in designing policies to this end.

Small industries require special advisory and extension services, analogous to the agricultural sector. Productivity improvement in this segment is a problem in most industrialized countries and innovative institutions such as have been developed in the Netherlands and Canada may be instructive. In both these countries, special organizations have been created, with government funds, specifically to promote the use of technical information in small firms. In each case field liaison officers provide a free advisory service, backed by industrial research laboratories and consultants.[1]

THE TRANSFER OF TECHNOLOGY

The process of transferring technological know-how from one culture to another, and specifically from an industrialized developed country to a less developed country, is as yet little understood, as equally are the obstacles to transfer and the best means of overcoming them. Under what circumstances must technology be tailored to suit physical, economic, and social conditions, or alternatively must local conditions be adapted to allow technology to be assimilated?

Within a given society technical change involves a process of invention, innovation, and diffusion of the new technique by imitation and acceptance. But an accepted technology transferred to another society involves commercial risks, a need for adaptation, and meets resistance to change, so that the transfer becomes more an innovative than an imitative process. To the recipient society it is new technology, however much accepted in the disseminating society. In general, technological transfer and diffusion is a cultural, social, and political process, and not just the imitation of manufactures. Clearly, given the inherent difficulties, transfer and diffusion cannot be expected as a spontaneous process, but require institutionalized channels of action.

Technical change affects the way men make a living, their social habits, their entire way of life, and is inevitably disruptive of established attitudes and practices. All societies have some

[1] *Government and technical innovation.* OECD, Paris, 1966, p. 48.

in-built resistance to change and a strong inclination to maintain the *status quo*. The capacity of a society to assimilate new technology depends on both its capacity to adapt the technology to its own conditions and its capacity to adapt itself to the needs of technology. Some technologies are readily accepted, as for example the cinema or aircraft transportation. Others, having a more immediate disruptive potential, may require a massive education programme and a much wider scientific literacy before acceptance. But this again is an area about which little is known.

The process integrates a large number of complementary elements, all of which are involved in effective transfer. These elements have been broadly grouped into three categories. 'To establish modern technology in an underdeveloped country, we need to change: social systems and human attitudes; knowledge and human skills; the physical implements in which modern technology is embodied.'[1] All these factors are complex and interrelated, but a successful strategy for development depends on being able to find means of overcoming the bottlenecks offering the primary resistance to change.

In many countries the tendency is to promote scientific and technological change from the top, assuming that the introduction of very advanced techniques in limited sectors of the economy will gradually filter down to all levels, eventually modernizing all sectors of the economy. By contrast, in China the policy of Mao Tse-tung aims first to equip the labour force with new technical skills—however rudimentary—and rely on the innovative abilities of skilled workers to generate technical progress. Modernization would thus be accomplished from the bottom up, as the technological capabilities of the workers became progressively more sophisticated.[2] In the classical Marxist view, productive forces have a great impact and influence on production relationships, playing in many respects a decisive role, though unable to change automatically the social structure of a society.

Adaptation of new technology to the context of operations in

---

[1] I. Svennilson: 'The Strategy of Transfer'. In *The transfer of technology to developing countries*, ed. by D. L. Spencer and A. Woroniak, Praeger, 1967, p. 176.

[2] Genevieve C. Dean: 'Science and the thoughts of Chairman Mao'. *New Scientist*, 12 February 1970, p. 298.

a less developed, low productivity economy may take place at
different levels.

1. The adjustment of machines or processes to a particular
   set of circumstances or needs.
2. Mastery of the technical knowledge related to a mechanism
   or technique, and its use to design more appropriate
   mechanisms and techniques.
3. Mastery of the analytical concepts of science and its
   research method, and their direct application to the needs
   and problems of the developing society.

A society's capacity to adapt itself to the requisites of advanced
technology and to adapt the advanced technology to its own
circumstances and objectives, as well as its capacity to innovate, will
depend in part on the intellectual skills, the acquired knowledge and
know-how, the problem solving competencies—in a word, on the
cognitions possessed by those who constitute that society.[1]

Recent studies have confirmed that technology transfer
becomes more difficult in so far as it has to include a wider
range of basic knowledge. The indications are that the greater
the differences between disseminator and recipient in respect of
technical and managerial skills, management and corporate
structure, and industrial environment, the greater the problems.
Any effective transfer requires a planned and sustained effort on
both sides.

Access to foreign technology and the cost of its acquisition
have often been described as major difficulties for LDCs, as
discussed for example at the two UNCTAD Conferences.[2] The
UN Economic and Social Council has initiated a series of
studies designed to throw more light on these questions.
'Technology transfer centres' have been proposed[3] to help
LDCs gain access to both patented and non-patented technologies, and to reduce foreign exchange costs, but no detailed
feasibility studies on such centres have yet been attempted.

[1] R. A. Solo: 'The capacity to assimilate an advanced technology'. *The American
Economic Review*, LVI, No. 2, May 1966, p. 91.
[2] United Nations Conference on Trade and Development, Second Session, New
Delhi, 1968.
[3] U.N. Advisory Committee on the Application of Science and Technology to
Development, Third Report, May 1966.

More liberal trade policies on the part of developed countries towards manufactured goods from LDCs would be a useful step forward.

In practice, where the environment encourages innovation, large firms seem to have relatively little difficulty in gaining access to required techniques. The main problems appear to relate to small and medium sized firms, which may require institutional help to identify and adapt the most appropriate technologies.

CHOICE OF TECHNOLOGY

The technologies of an advanced industrialized society have been developed in response to the needs and conditions of that society, particularly with regard to markets—normally large, and with comparatively high incomes—and to resources and their comparative costs—high labour costs, but an adequate supply of capital and strong managerial and technical skills. It would be remarkable, therefore, if they proved optimal for a less developed society with plentiful unskilled labour, but a shortage of capital and skills, and usually small low-income markets.

The extent to which known technologies can be adapted to suit local conditions is limited, and adaptation itself may be expensive. Both from the point of view of employment, and on strictly economic grounds, there would seem to be scope for the development of new technologies better suited to local costs and resources—often described as appropriate or intermediate technologies.

But the choice of technology is a decision normally taken at the level of the business enterprise, and in practice only an advanced technology may be available, or at least readily accessible. The industrialist, or his consultant advisers, may be familiar with only Western sources. This apart, there may be other factors urging a decision towards capital-intensive equipment. In some cases new techniques may reduce both capital and labour requirements per unit of output. The quality of product necessary for export competitiveness, even within regional markets, may be achievable only with capital-intensive methods. As technical standards rise, opportunities for the substitution of unskilled labour for capital usually diminish rapidly.[1] In some industries, such as fertilizers, steel and power generation, plants and processes are highly scale sensitive, and low production costs require large-scale high-capital units.

In addition, the relative costs of capital and labour may be distorted at the enterprise decision-making level. Tax allowances on capital equipment, or subsidized interest rates may lower apparent capital costs, while inflated wage rates, high redundancy costs, and over-powerful unions may discourage labour-intensive methods. Governments may need to adapt fiscal policies to encourage correct economic decisions by business managers.

The predominant argument in favour of appropriate technology is the need for employment, and depends on the fact that the capital cost of most production goods is as much and often more in LDCs earning $100 per head, as in industrialized countries earning $2,000 per head. In many countries the population is increasing by 3 per cent per annum. Assuming that only one in three of these eventually require employment, in a hypothetical country of 10 million people, this means that about 100,000 new jobs have to be created each year. Population control is a necessity for the long-term future, but cannot have an immediate effect. Suppose the hypothetical country has a GNP of $100 per head and a net investment rate of 10 per cent, then total annual net investment in all sectors will be $10 per head or $100,000,000. For 100,000 new jobs this gives an average of $1,000 per job.

The capital cost required to create a work place in a modern industry in a developed country can be as high as $50,000 but on average may be about $5,000. For economic reasons, part of the investment in manufacturing in LDCs must go into large-scale, capital-intensive industries. To come anywhere near an answer to the employment problem, therefore, most new jobs in LDCs must be created at a capital cost well below $1,000 per head.[2]

In the rural areas of many LDCs even a few tens of dollars in capital equipment, such as improved hand tools or simple

[1] J. Baranson: *Role of science and technology in advanced development of newly industrialising states*. Socio-Economic Planning Sciences, Vol. 3, p. 351, 1969. Prepared under a contract with the U.S. Dept. of State.
[2] Lord Blackett, op. cit. No. II, p. 32.

machines for the local processing of natural products might increase production very appreciably. Some local market needs may be met with quite unsophisticated machinery or processes. So one has a complete spectrum of the intensity of industrialization, ranging from $50,000 worth of capital for each operative in big chemical and steel plants, to some tens of dollars per worker in a small workshop. Each country must work out for itself the best 'shape' of this investment spectrum for its own conditions. In this, as in many other aspects of development, Japan's history offers an instructive example, with many industries up to the 1950s comprising a highly labour-intensive sector supplying intermediary parts to large modern capital-intensive plants.

Most modern technologies have been developed under the conditions of the advanced industrial societies, and tend to be relevant to the upper ranges of this spectrum. The unemployment problem in LDCs is a challenge to scientists, technologists, engineers, and entrepreneurs throughout the world to develop modern efficient technologies more appropriate to the middle and lower ranges of the spectrum.

RESEARCH INSTITUTIONS

What has been said so far indicates clearly the major roles of research in a developing country, in so far as local resources allow.

1. To help select and adapt existing scientific and technological knowledge to meet specific local needs.
2. To maintain contact with developments elsewhere of potential local importance.
3. To augment existing knowledge in fields of potential relevance, with particular emphasis on those areas which, for various reasons, are not or cannot be properly studied elsewhere, as in relation to specific biological or mineral resources, climatic and soil conditions, or social problems.
4. As far as possible within the limits of the foregoing, as a necessary activity in the training of scientific and technical personnel and their teachers.

It has also been indicated that under the present production structure and economic environment, industry in the LDCs is unlikely to make much direct contribution to R and D, though the experience of the developed countries underlines the importance of close links between research and industry for effective application.

Most LDCs have therefore set up research institutions which are wholly or partly government financed. But it has been frequently noted that many of these scientific research institutes play little part in national development, and are often engaged in work more relevant to the problems and interests of developed countries. Through their science policy organizations, governments can ensure that due priority in the allocation of limited human and financial resources is given to research programmes related to economic and social needs. LDCs cannot afford more than a small effort in research isolated from the practical needs of the community. Even in countries such as the U.K. basic science accounts for only about 10 per cent of the total budget for R and D, and so amounts to not more than 0·3 per cent of the GNP. This raises the difficult problem of the attitudes of scientists, some of whom tend to over-emphasize the importance in the short run of fundamental research and prefer not to become involved in the practical problems of industry and agriculture. Changing these attitudes will take time and effort, but the process may be helped by encouraging interconnecting links between the universities and research institutes, industry and agriculture, and the Administration. Mobility of trained personnel can also be useful, but may be hindered by administrative obstacles, such as inflexible pension schemes.

In this general context, the approach of the director of the Central Leather Research Institute in India, who is also honorary professor of leather technology at the University of Madras, is very relevant.

The most important factors in the effective utilisation of research are the potential users and the institutions which supply the research. It is the potential users' capacity to appreciate and actually utilise the relevant technology made available by research that is decisive. Equally decisive are the planning, organisation and management of research in the research institutions, and its development and sale.[1]

[1] Y. Nayudamma: 'Promoting the industrial application of research in an underdeveloped country'. *Minerva*, V, No. 3, Spring 1967, p. 323.

In direct conflict with the above views, it has been argued that, at their present stage of development, under-developed countries should encourage as much good quality research as possible, regardless of relevance.[1] Selection of research topics on an economic return basis is held to be premature, and first-class scientists should be allowed to follow their own interests, so as to ensure international and hence national status to the scientific and technological effort, set standards of excellence, and help to reduce the 'brain drain'.

This may perhaps be a valid argument for the brilliant highly self-motivated few, unless perhaps very expensive 'big science' equipment is involved. But most of the remainder should find satisfaction in mission-oriented research organizations, provided they are well organized and directed, and are integrated into the national development effort. Some research organizations have been described as bureaucratic and authoritarian institutions, tending towards the repetition of more or less stereotyped mediocre work.[2] The factors which encourage or stunt creative productivity among scientists and engineers merit careful study.

An important consideration in research organization is the threshold size for effective work. Many research laboratories are small, ill-equipped, and poorly funded, and cannot be expected to make a useful contribution. Effective work on important problems requires a range of skills and increasingly an interdisciplinary approach. Few scientists are able to work alone, and they benefit from the stimulation of close contacts with fellow-workers. Adequate technical support is also an important element in research productivity, and expensive items of equipment may be essential. Probably the most significant factor in work quality and value is the experienced research director or team leader. Such people are unusually rare in the early stages of an under-developed country.

All these aspects indicate the importance of a minimum critical size of research effort. There is as yet no general basis for determining this critical size, which is of course related to the

[1] See, for example, J. A. Sabato: 'Some comments on the problem of the best utilisation of scientific and technical resources'. *Applied Science and World Economy*, U.S. House of Representatives, 1968.

[2] T. Ree: 'Interrelationship between research at applied research organisations and academic institutions'. *International Symposium on Development of Industrial Research in Korea*, Institute of Science and Technology, 1968, p. 40.

general environment and the type of problems being tackled. It is interesting to note that Imperial Chemical Industries Limited regard an annual expenditure of £1,000,000 p.a., involving about 100 graduates, with their supporting staff, as a minimum for a worthwhile R and D effort in a giant firm covering a highly complex field. Despite the scale, few useful results of major importance would be expected during the first ten years— research organizations require long-term commitments. In a narrower, more specialized field a smaller R and D effort would be viable but excessive fragmentation must be avoided. On the basis of U.K. costs, even a small group of five research scientists, with their appropriate supporting staff and research expenses, would cost about £50,000 p.a.

This gives some indication of the size of investment involved, particularly when it is remembered that carrying a new idea through to a market product or process will require a much larger expenditure. With their limited resources of research management, qualified staff and finance, most LDCs can afford a very limited number of multi-disciplinary research centres. It is therefore vital to consider carefully the areas where they can make the maximum contribution.

It also suggests the importance for smaller countries with severely limited means, as for example in parts of Africa, to pool their efforts in fields of common interest. But regional research output is of little value without some base in each country which can take up and use the results. The primary interest, therefore, is for each country to develop its own scientific potential, if necessary with the help of technical assistance programmes. But this should not prevent some concentration of efforts by mutual agreement, and for mutual benefits.

However well organized and effective, the total research effort in the less developed world will be small in comparison with that in the developed world, probably in the ratio of some 1:30. While the results of some of the developed world's R and D appears in less developed countries in the form of modern equipment and new processes, very little of it is specifically concerned with the problems of the developing world. Individual industrialized countries and various international agencies have given significant help with the creation and improvement of scientific facilities within the less developed world, and notable contributions have been made by the International Research Centres of the Ford and Rockefeller Foundations. But much more needs to be done.

The Pearson Commission has recommended that aid-suppliers devote a significant share of their R and D resources and facilities to projects specifically related to problems of developing countries. It has been proposed

that targets for 1972 should amount to 5 per cent of public expenditure for research and development (of aid-suppliers), of which at least half should be spent in developing countries, and that a special procedure be applied to the United States, where spending for research and development is considerably higher than elsewhere. It is therefore suggested that the United States be asked to match the total pledges of other main donors.

Similar proposals have been made by the United Nations Advisory Committee on the Application of Science and Technology to Development. The Commission has estimated that by 1975 these recommendations will amount to over $500,000,000 p.a. to be spent in LDCs, and an equal amount in developed countries on R and D relevant to the problems of LDCs. The effective redeployment of research funds on this scale, and the supply of appropriately specialized manpower required to use them, obviously present immense difficulties.

It is important to ensure that any such efforts are not only relevant to the problems and recognized needs of LDCs, but fit into their own development plans. They must strengthen not discourage the growing scientific potential in the LDCs. New mechanisms to harness the R and D facilities of the rich countries to development problems will have to be devised. The Commission has recommended 'that industrialized countries assist in the establishment of international and regional centres for scientific and technological research in developing countries, designed to serve the community of the developing world and specializing in distinct fields of research and their application'. The proposed Canadian International Development Research Centre, which is designed to 'bring to bear the techniques and resources of science and technology on the fundamental problems of under-developed countries', should prove a useful step in this direction.

Stronger bilateral links between research institutions and universities in developing and developed countries can also be useful where there is a genuine mutual interest. A notable example is the Korean Institute of Science and Technology, which is in a sisterhood relationship with the Battelle Memorial Institute in the U.S.A.

THE ROLE OF UNIVERSITIES

With the shortage of qualified scientists, technologists, engineers, and technicians as one of the most critical limiting factors in the effective application of science and technology in LDCs, universities and other institutions of higher education have a decisive role to play in development. In addition to qualified personnel for industry, agriculture, and administration, extra staff is required to expand the universities to meet future demands, and science teachers are needed at primary and secondary school levels to promote a more general awareness of science in the community. Apart from a direct contribution to education, including the use of modern educational technologies, universities have an important role in helping to create a social climate favourable to development.

Except for a number of long-standing universities in Latin America and India, the majority of the universities in LDCs are relatively new. But many of them have used the older traditional type of European university as a model, and have sometimes tended to foster an exclusive *élite*, out of touch with the local people and national needs. In some countries the universities have been rightly concerned with maintaining their autonomy against threats of political interference, but academic freedom and university autonomy need not pre-empt active involvement in national development. Evidently the education system must be adapted to suit local needs. In the words of Sir Eric Ashby, 'higher education is unlikely to bring its full benefit to a country unless its content, emphasis, and balance between different fields of study, are adapted to the indigenous culture and the nation's economic environment'.[1]

Within the faculties, while the importance of science as an

[1] Sir Eric Ashby: *Universities: British, Indian, African.* Weidenfeld & Nicolson, 1966, p. 142.

4

intellectual discipline and a cultural activity is well recognized, its value as a source of national material wealth is often neglected. A scientist is judged by the acclaim of his peers on the basis of his published work. Under these circumstances, faculty staff engaged in research, often in relative local isolation, tend to follow the dictates and fashions of the world's scientific community, which is overwhelmingly of the developed world. Research work is thus frequently more relevant to the problems of the developed world than to local needs. Overseas training may merely exacerbate these tendencies.

In some countries heavy training and administration loads, and the need to augment incomes by outside work, make research or even contact with research virtually impossible. The teachers slowly lose touch with developments in their subject, and the faculties tend to become tradition-bound, compartmentalized into narrow disciplines, rapidly losing any remaining creative spirits. Such a situation cannot be improved overnight, and it has sometimes been found necessary to allow an old institution to decline, and concentrate efforts on a new start.

Strong links are needed with research organizations, and with industry and agriculture, and scientists in universities should be encouraged to participate in joint research programmes. Universities can build up confidence with the industrial and commercial community by providing useful services, such as standards testing, and by contract research, even though this may incur some restrictions. Such contacts with future employers, supplemented by continuing concern with past graduates, can help universities better to adapt curricula to take account of the fact that the majority of the scientists and technologists produced will be most usefully employed in agriculture, extension services, production and management, rather than in research.

Whatever the economic system, managers and entrepreneurs have a vital role in making the most of a nation's resources. Training in this field can lead to considerable improvements in the effectiveness of performance, but is often a neglected area. Modern management techniques as used in industrial countries may need to be modified to suit the particular social and cultural circumstances in an LDC, and universities can make a significant contribution in this area.

The importance of rural development in LDCs, with their predominantly agricultural populations, has already been discussed. Some universities are now playing an active part in rural development, such as for example the Ahmadu Bello University in Northern Nigeria. Dr. I. S. Audu of Ahmadu Bello once quoted an old Nigerian proverb which says, 'The owner of the house knows where the roof leaks.' He concluded, 'That is where we need to work. That is what needs to be done.'

II Science Policy

INTRODUCTION

Science policy is concerned essentially with the optimal use of science and technology as agents of economic growth and social development, taking the latter to include the advance of knowledge.

From an initial concern with a policy for science in the strict sense, in recent years the concept and practices of science policy have evolved rapidly. The term is now taken to cover science, including social and behavioural sciences, as well as natural sciences, technology, and engineering. The Director of Scientific Affairs for OECD[1] has observed that in the initial enthusiasm for science policy in relation to national economic growth goals, there was a somewhat naïve tendency to assume that more research was the main requirement in assuring more rapid growth, but it is now recognized that many other factors are involved. Hence attention has passed from an easy advocacy of more science for more growth to concern for a deeper understanding of the nature of the innovation process and the conditions which favour it.

UNESCO, the U.N. agency responsible for advising LDCs on science policy, has proposed the following definition. 'The sum of the legislative and executive measures taken to increase, organise and use the national scientific and technological potential, with the object of achieving the country's overall development aims and enhancing its position in the world.'[2] In this context, the national scientific and technological potential is taken to comprise 'all organised resources a country has at its sovereign disposal for the purpose of discovery, invention and innovation, and for the study of national and international problems that science and its applications involve'.

[1] Alexander King: 'Science policy, economic growth and the quality of life'. Text of the Sixth Annual Science of Science Foundation Lecture, *Science Policy News*, 2, No. 1, July 1970.

[2] UNESCO: *The application of science and technology to the development of Asia. Basic data and considerations.* SC/CASTASIA 3, p. 116, 8 May 1968.

Science policy is thus seen to have two main aspects: the long-term development of a national scientific and technological potential, and the most effective use of this potential to meet development needs. Even this broad definition might be questioned as it fails to stress the importance of making best use of the scientific knowledge and technological know-how obtainable from other countries, through technical assistance programmes and direct transfer.

Few developed countries, if any, have a clear science policy in these broad terms, but rather they have an agglomerate of many partial science and technology policies, more or less co-ordinated at the centre. To some extent this is an inevitable result of the large number of controlling forces at play, but in LDCs, where typically the financial control of scientific activities and of economic development is largely in government hands, a coherent science policy is perhaps more feasible and almost certainly more necessary.

DEVELOPMENT GOALS AND SCIENCE POLICY

In principle, a national science policy should be a reflection of long-term national goals and objectives, and the overall economic and social development plan designed to achieve these aims. Only within the context of such an overall plan can a valid science policy be formulated.

The plan will have been developed, more or less systematically, from a confrontation of what is considered desirable as a future national position, and what is considered achievable, given the internal and external constraints. This indicates immediately the importance of a continuous two-way inter-action between science planning and development planning. Any assessment of future possibilities, and appropriate development strategies, must be based on an analysis of national strengths and weaknesses, which should take into account the potential contribution that science and technology can offer in the development of latent resources and the more productive use of known resources. Combining a knowledge of scientific and technological trends, and such information as is available on national resources, national planners can apply technological forecasting techniques to extrapolate to possible futures. The use of science and technology can thus extend the horizons and offer a wider range of options to the socio-economic planners. Science planning, therefore, needs to become an integral part of overall development planning. The situation is, of course, not static, and the whole should form a dynamic system able to respond to new knowledge, new information and changing circumstances.

But setting national goals and determining priorities, within the limits of available resources, are evidently political decisions to be taken at the highest governmental level, and are not the prerogatives of scientists *per se*. The concern of the scientific community must be to ensure that the decisions are based on the fullest and most accurate advice available, and that scientific resources are then applied in the most effective way.

THE SCOPE OF SCIENCE PLANNING

Within the guidelines of the overall development plan, an operational strategy must be devised to cover the two main functions of science policy—the development of the scientific and technological potential, and its effective use. No country has the means to be strong in every field, and this strategy has therefore to be selective. Taking into account the present and future importance of the various sectors as contributors to national wealth, social well-being, employment, security and so on, particular needs for the development of natural resources, comparative advantages and weaknesses, an attempt must be made to select the areas in which to concentrate efforts and develop a strong capability, able to make full use of all available technology and know-how, whether from indigenous or foreign sources. Outside these areas the capability will be correspondingly weak, with greater reliance on traditional know-how. Without this deliberately selective approach, the application of science and technology is likely to be a random effort.

In many LDCs, science in the narrow sense is relatively much more developed than technology or engineering. The science growth points may be in the universities, which are jealous guardians of their autonomy, and where for historical and social reasons the emphasis is usually on fundamental research. In so far as the need for science policy is accepted at all, it is seen by many scientists as a policy in favour of science, particularly fundamental science. Under such circumstances science policy has tended to be concerned very largely with fundamental scientific research, and sometimes with highly advanced technologies, often of little relevance to the national economy. The economic and management aspects of technological innovation and diffusion, especially at a more prosaic level, have been neglected, though potentially more significant and more rewarding socially.

Correctly, science policy is concerned with the application of existing knowledge, augmented as found necessary by indigenous research or by importation from other countries, to the production of goods and services, and therefore covers the whole chain of research, development, and invention, through to innovation and diffusion. Science policy which is solely concerned with R and D programmes will be of little practical value, as the translation of results into economic uses—the dissemination, innovation, and diffusion stages—are often the weakest links in the chain. Appropriate institutional arrangements and inter-relationships between universities, research centres and the economic sectors, are needed to ensure not only that R and D programmes are relevant to objectives, but that successful results are followed through to practical application. Science policy thus overlaps into such fields as agricultural extension services, industrial incentives, and the analysis of market requirements. This is especially important in LDCs, where the economic structure does not always itself create a demand for research and innovation, and governments have a more active role to play in promoting innovation and productivity improvement than may be necessary in already industrialized market economies.

In the development of a scientific and technological potential, the main limiting factor other than investment capital is likely to be the lack of qualified personnel. Here again, science policy is concerned not only with the supply and training of research scientists, but also with the training and distribution of scientists, technologists, engineers, and technicians in production, marketing, and public administration, and most particularly the development of technically-minded managers and entrepreneurs. The general level of vocational training and the scientific awareness of the population as a whole are also highly relevant. Evidently, science policy and education policy are closely inter-related, ideally representing specific aspects of a single coherent development programme.

ORGANIZATION FOR SCIENCE POLICY

The organizational arrangements for science policy fall into three distinct and separate functions—formulation of strategy, administration, and operational control.

The formulation of strategy is of necessity a highly-centralized function, at the national level. As this level calls for decision-making in relation to national goals and priorities, and the resolution of conflicting claims on resources, the ultimate decision centre for science policy should be at Cabinet or equivalent level, and typically takes the form of a Ministerial Committee, often headed by or reporting to the Prime Minister or President. Such a body requires the best available technical advice and support, which is normally provided by an advisory committee, with supporting specialist advisory groups and backed by a permanent science secretariat, responsible for formulating plans and for liaison with the overall planning and budgetary functions.

Most developed countries and several LDCs have set up organizations of this sort. The actual form varies considerably, but may be illustrated by the situation in Japan, where planning for the economy and planning for science and technology are brought together in the advisory and administrative system of the Office of the Prime Minister. Two advisory bodies, the Economic Deliberation Council and the Council for Science and Technology, are provided with secretarial services by two major agencies for that Office: the Economic Planning Agency and the Science and Technology Agency. The importance attached to science policy, and to economic planning, may to some extent be judged by the fact that the three agencies with similar status deal with subjects of considerable national importance: defence, public safety, and Hokkaido development. Science policy is considered by the Cabinet members in the Council for Science and Technology. While this council is not organizationally related to the Cabinet, the presence of four

Cabinet Members (Education, Finance, Economic Planning Agency, Science and Technology Agency) under the chairmanship of the Prime Minister makes it effectively a Cabinet-level organ. In addition, it includes the President of the Science Council of Japan, and five other persons of 'learning and experience' appointed by the Prime Minister, supplemented by additional temporary appointments, as well as by the presence on sub-committees of numerous 'specialist' members.[1]

There is, however, no standard pattern of organization, and in any specific case detailed arrangements will depend on the size of the country and its stage of development, its accepted political and administrative structures, and on the personnel available. Some form of science policy organization can be useful even in a country where the indigenous research effort is relatively small, to provide a policy framework within which to co-ordinate technical assistance, graduate and post-graduate training, technology imports, and the build up of the scientific and technological infrastructure.

Personnel for such an organization will be a major problem for most LDCs. At the advisory committee level, it is evidently important to enlist the best economists, scientists, industrialists, and agriculturalists in government service, the universities, and the economic sectors, so as to achieve a balanced and comprehensive view of national problems, and constructive thinking on future opportunities. In some LDCs most of the scientists are to be found within the universities, and the organization may become excessively academic in complexion. But the management of applied science and technology cannot be left to a small group of academic scientists, however gifted they may be in their individual fields. It requires also the full participation of individuals experienced in politics, economics, management, and engineering. To avoid the dangers of entrenched opinions and limited perspective, the spectrum needs to be as broad as possible.

The permanent staff of the secretariat also needs to be of high calibre, as they will be required to undertake, or supervise, a broad range of supporting surveys and studies. They will probably have to be taken from a very limited supply of scientists, and this can be justified only by the more effective

---

[1] OECD: *Reviews of national science policy—Japan*. Paris, 1967, p. 75 *et seq.*

use then made of the remainder. Hence it is important to keep the science policy organization as simple as possible, in relation to the overall science and technology effort. There is little to be gained if the few good scientists a country may have spend most of their time in committee rooms. A top-heavy bureaucracy can easily develop unless the overhead costs of planning science are kept in line with total expenditure on science, with a ceiling of at most 5 per cent.

Below this overall planning level, institution arrangements are needed, still on a national basis, to put into effect the policy decisions through co-ordinated activities within each sector. Below this again, at the operational level, comes the network of research organizations, institutes, universities, extension and advisory units, and auxiliary services, where scientific and technological work is actually carried out. While the broad decisions of science policy are necessarily made at the centre, experience has shown the value of decentralized detailed control and programming at the operational level. Given their mission in the overall plan, the individual organizations are likely to be most effective if left free to carry out their work with the minimum of day-to-day interference.

Throughout the system, an important aspect is the need for flexibility in both the long and short term, allowing for re-direction of effort in response to events. Research is inherently unpredictable, and there must be continual assessments of effectiveness, and an efficient, speedy feedback into the planning system for adjustment to be made. 'It is becoming fairly clear that similarities and differences between the science policy planning systems in the various countries lie not so much in the initial planning process as in the nature and effectiveness of these feedback control mechanisms.'[1]

In addition to the governmental instruments for science policy, mechanisms which will allow the non-governmental scientific-engineering community to criticize government pro-grammes constructively and advise the government about needs and opportunities in research and education are im-portant. These may include an 'Academy' which is close to government but not part of it, and in some cases an 'Association for the Advancement of Science'. 'The most effective "mixture"

[1] UNESCO: op. cit., p. 120.

of organizations will vary greatly from country to country and will also vary with time. Each nation must select and support that mixture of governmental and non-governmental structure and activities which it believes will come closest to fulfilling its needs.'[1]

EFFECTIVENESS OF SCIENCE POLICY

While many countries have now attempted to establish science policy organizations, even where they do exist they are rarely fully integrated with development planning. In Latin America, for example, only Argentina and Venezuela have organizations which are achieving any significant measure of co-ordination between science policy and the national development plan. More often science policy is conceived in the restricted framework of budgetary allocations for research, and the responsible body, perhaps a National Council for Scientific Research, is essentially concerned with the development and promotion of science for its own sake, for which state support is justified on the intrinsic value of science.

The situation has been described by Victor Urquidi, President of the College of Mexico, in an address on 31 December 1968.

The present situation of science and technology in Latin America should be of great immediate concern. Research and development, and academic scientific formation, have been the result of more or less spontaneous, low-level efforts, individualism and narrow objectives. There is no notable concentration of effort but rather a good deal of dispersion and wastage. On the one hand, the universities, where most research is done, hardly relate to the needs of the community, especially in the case of industry. In so far as national development policies exist in a few countries, research and development are not integrated into those policies. Government support for scientific research is generally weak mainly as a result of a lack of appreciation of its importance, but also because of insufficient communication between government and the scientific community.[2]

Similar conditions may be found in many other countries, and are likely to continue unless positive steps are taken to

[1] Harrison Brown: 'Science policy and economic development'. U.S. National Academy of Sciences, 1968.
[2] Victor Urquidi: 'Science policy and national economic development in Latin America'. Presented at a Symposium on Science, Technology and Latin American development, Dallas, 31 December 1968.

bridge the communications gap between government policy-makers and scientists, and to define the role of the scientific community in socio-economic development. Obviously of importance here are the different attitudes and motivations on either side, which may reflect historical, social, and cultural patterns, but closer working relationships and increased involvement of scientists at policy levels should help to alleviate the situation.

Even where a science policy organization has been created with appropriate duties and responsibilities clearly specified in the terms of reference, the organization may not function effectively in the early stages. Essentially, a science policy organization may be regarded as a communications network. It takes time to acquire the strength and confidence, and to develop the formal and informal communications and contacts, necessary for an effective body.

More commonly, through lack of policies and central direction, research organizations tend to be self-perpetuating, and may receive support with little regard to the value of their results. Funds often depend more on the strength of personality of the research director, rather than on the particular contribution to the total effort. Some organizations may be involved in work of little or no relevance to national needs, beyond a marginal contribution to training, which could be more economically obtained in some other way. The sheer weight of the scientific effort in the developed world draws scientists in LDCs, working in relative isolation, towards questions considered interesting and important by the international scientific community, but not necessarily having any bearing on their own national or regional problems.

Quite an extensive research organization may grow up in this way, out of balance with national requirements, and often neglecting major areas of considerable strategic importance in economic development. In Pakistan, for example, it has been pointed out[1] that expenditure on nuclear energy research during 1962–7 amounted to ten times that spent on all other applied fields, such as jute and fish; which together earn some $300,000,000 in foreign exchange. Pakistan has also received

[1] M. ul Haq: 'Planning investment in scientific research'. *Development Digest*, IV, No. 4, January 1967, p. 66.

assistance in setting up a modern heart clinic.[1] But most of the benefits of advances in nuclear energy or heart surgery are obtainable from the developed countries, while applied research on the natural resources of LDCs must be done by these countries. Just as industrialized countries are investigating synthetic substitutes for jute, jute producers need to explore the possibilities of new uses and a broader market for the natural material. In many countries environmental studies are given little attention, and the earth sciences, which are basic to the use of natural resources, are frequently disregarded.

Frequently, too, the research effort is dissipated in a large number of small units, with inadequate supporting services, which need to be brought together in a small number of centres to be truly effective. In Lebanon, for example, it was found that 65 per cent of the research units had less than five research workers, and an annual budget of only £25,000 p.a.[2] The reorganization of such a structure can be done intelligently only in the context of an overall plan.

EXPENDITURE ON R AND D

As is well known, the more advanced developed countries typically spend some 2 to 3 per cent of their Gross National Product on R and D, and, though considerable problems of definition are involved, this ratio is often used for broad inter-country comparisons of scientific efforts. LDCs, on the other hand, may spend from less than 0·05 per cent to at most 0·5 per cent of GNP, though the figure is rarely known with any accuracy, and sometimes not at all. Targets are frequently set towards a substantial increase in this expenditure by LDCs. The 1968 Conference on the Application of Science and Technology to the Development of Asia (CASTASIA),[3] for example recommended to the participating governments a minimum level of total national expenditure on R and D of 1 per cent of the Gross National Product 'as soon as possible, hopefully not later

[1] Prestige projects are of course to be found in every country and many have considerable political importance. But it is as well to be clear just why the expenditure is being incurred.

[2] UNESCO: *Liban—La recherche scientifique et le plan quinquennal.* Paris, September 1968. Report by Dr. P. Piganiol.

[3] UNESCO: *CASTASIA. Conclusions and recommendations.* Paris, 10 June 1969.

than 1980'. Similar recommendations have been made in Africa and Latin America.

But it must be recognized that there is some danger in such blanket targets. The expenditure refers only to R and D, which is but part of the total science and technology activity, itself only one of the many factors in the development process. Though it is sometimes given the aura of a panacea, increased R and D alone evidently will not increase the rate of growth. Given very limited human financial resources the allocation to R and D has to be made at the expense of some other activity. When determining optimum allocations it is useful to bear in mind the concept of 'opportunity costs'—that for any specific action the essential cost is always what must be foregone in order to do it.

Education is to some extent in competition with R and D for the available human and financial resources. A high rate of expansion of secondary and higher science education opportunities will absorb much of its own product, leaving few scientists of adequate calibre to contribute directly to economic growth. At the same time technical personnel are vitally necessary in production and supporting services, marketing, management, and administration. The more effective application of existing and acquired technologies may well depend more on a wider use of scientists and technologists in this way, than on increased R and D.

Despite their importance in the efficient use of resources, supporting scientific and technological services are often neglected in LDCs. Unfortunately, unlike R and D, there are as yet no generally accepted definitions, and useful data on expenditure are therefore limited. One tentative definition includes the following activities:

Scientific library and information services;
Scientific testing and standards services;
Museums, zoological and botanical gardens;
Geological, geophysical, meteorological and natural resources, survey work, including mapping;
General purpose social and economic data collection;
Technical and scientific advisory, consultancy and extension services, including patent offices, and related activities.[1]

[1] The Sussex Group: *Science, technology and underdevelopment: The case for reform.* University of Sussex, 1970, p. 7.

Detailed aspects of some of these services are discussed more fully in subsequent chapters, and there can be no doubt that they have an essential role in industrial and agricultural development. Though international statistics for comparative studies are sadly lacking, a much larger allocation of funds to these services than the total R and D budget would normally be justified.

With regard to R and D itself, the sum of expenditure is of course not the only criterion. Of greater importance may be the fields in which R and D are carried out and their relevance to economic growth, and also the distribution of expenditure between fundamental research, applied research, and engineering development. The development stages, requiring pilot plants and workshop facilities or experimental farms, are much more expensive than laboratory research, but are equally necessary. Regard must be had, therefore, to the distribution of effort within the R and D allocation, and the facilities required.

Furthermore, as discussed in Chapter I, in developed countries R and D has been estimated to account for only 5 to 10 per cent of the total costs which must be incurred in successful innovation. While not all R and D will lead to innovation, it is certain that the later stages will require much greater resources than are required for R and D alone. It is evidently wasteful to undertake research unless these funds, and the management resources required to apply the results, can be made available when needed. Equally important, the links in the innovation chain must have been established to ensure that the results accord with market or social needs. To quote again from the CASTASIA report

measurements of expenditures do not provide any information about the exploitation of the results of scientific work by the economy through the process of technological innovation. It is reasonable to suppose that, as expenditures reach sizeable proportions, national authorities will see to it that proper use is made of these funds. This however has to be assessed, not assumed.[1]

A network of structural links and inter-relationships between research centres, auxiliary and extension services, and the 'customers' has to be built up and maintained. Effective

[1] UNESCO: *Basic data and considerations.* Op. cit., p. 144.

linking between research and production is a problem even within a single firm, and it is a particularly difficult problem in LDCs which has often been neglected in science policy organizations. Where market pressures for innovation and productivity improvements are weak and ineffective, the responsibility for developing these networks falls on the government. In this context, the experience of centrally planned economies may be relevant to the problems of some LDCs.

The traditional Soviet arrangement for innovation forms a chain linking academy research institute to industrial research institution to design bureau to factory, corresponding roughly to the stages of fundamental research, applied research, engineering development, and implementation. But according to an OECD study of science policy in the U.S.S.R.,[1] while the system of planning and organization was effective, under Soviet conditions, in the early stages of industrialization, it now offers serious obstacles to technical innovation and its diffusion. The study distinguished, with admitted over-simplification, four major sets of obstacles to technical innovation in the Soviet R and D system, which the central authorities are attempting to overcome.

1. Insufficient availability of development facilities.
2. The reluctance of the factory to innovate, owing to the impact of central planning.
3. The administrative barriers between the R and D system and industrial production, in turn reinforced by the system of planning.
4. The inter-departmental barriers to the co-ordination of R and D.

Soviet accounts of R and D strongly emphasize that there is a research/development imbalance, as insufficient resources are put into development compared to those put into research, so that the main bottleneck in Soviet R and D is the relative un-availability of facilities for manufacturing and proving proto-types. The tendency of the research institutes and design bureaux to neglect the problems of the application of their work in production, coupled with the shortage of development facilities and supplies of new materials, makes it much more

[1] OECD: *Science Policy in the USSR*. Paris, 1969, p. 435 *et seq.*

SCIENCE POLICY 47

difficult to bring new products into production. To improve the situation, stronger links have been advocated between the research institute, the design bureau, and the group of factories requiring their services.

Thus great care is needed in determining the appropriate expenditure on R and D and its breakdown. In most industrialized market economies the 'science budget', in any total sense, is not predetermined. Much research is in any cafe financed by private industry, and so beyond the control so government, though it may be affected by fiscal policies. Private research in industrial firms is as yet rare in LDCs, and almost all research except for some in large foreign firms is government financed and carried out in government research organizations or in the universities. Generally speaking, government R and D expenditure in developed countries is determined within the portfolio of each department, as the best means of attaining its specific functional objectives. R and D may be considered as one way of meeting a goal, and as such is an investment to be economically justified, as any other expenditure in relation to the anticipated results. This will of course raise problems of the unpredictability of research, but as research proceeds into development, predictability increases, as also do costs, and increasingly rigorous cost-benefit analyses can be applied. Countries with sufficient resources may allocate additional funds to non-oriented basic research, normally in the hope of some long-term returns, including national prestige, but this may be hard to justify in the poorer and smaller LDCs.

These various demands will finally need to be brought together and adjusted in accordance with national priorities and the limited resources, including manpower and facilities, which are available to meet them. To help decision-making in the allocation of resources in applied science and technology a range of techniques have been, and are still being developed. Any one technique, however, tends to take a partial view of the problem, so that it is advisable to use several techniques and gain a compounded interpretation of the results. But though useful as guidelines, the subject is as yet too little understood for too much weight to be attached to these results. As observed by the OECD's Director of Scientific Affairs, 'Although the complex problem of resource allocation to research has not yet any

5

rational solution, discussions between scientists, economists and policy makers on the policy councils have placed it on a basis of informed common sense which is an undoubted improvement.'[1]

In making these decisions, it must be remembered that the importation and adaptation of foreign technology is frequently an alternative to indigenous research. LDCs will inevitably have to depend heavily in the foreseeable future on imported technology, and need to discover the means to make fullest use of such technology. The obstacles to diffusion and dissemination may need to be studied and appropriate institutions devised, but evidently this is a process which merits attention.

The dangers of over-reliance on imported technology are generally recognized. On the one hand, a government may take the availability of foreign technology to mean that no indigenous science structure is necessary. This in turn can lead to a misuse of local resources, a frustrated science community, and a serious brain drain problem. On the other hand, as the foreign exchange costs of technology imports rise, perhaps for machinery parts and raw materials as well as royalties and fees, governments may place restrictions on imports and forfeit the growth opportunities foreign technology can represent. Clearly a judicious control of expenditure on foreign technology is required, while the development of a complementary local science structure is encouraged. This is but one important aspect of science policy.

Though not all foreign technology involves royalty payments or patents fees, payments overseas under these heads provides the most convenient index of expenditure on science and technology outside the national system. The level of expenditure which will be acceptable for technology imports will depend on many factors, but, given adequate and effective controls, it can be much more important in the short term than R and D. According to the CASTASIA Report, 'If countries of the Asian region are aiming at economic growth through a scientifically based industrial development, then they would be expected to devote to the importation of technology financial resources at least equal to, if not many times greater than, the ones devoted to the performance of their own research and development.'[2]

[1] Alexander King: op. cit.
[2] UNESCO: *Basic data and considerations*: Op. cit., p. 156.

This obviously raises political as well as economic questions, which must be taken into account in formulating science policy.

In sum, R and D is only one part of the total expenditure on scientific and technological activities, and an over-emphasis on R and D targets may draw attention away from the importance of building up a complete scientific and technological service infrastructure, controlled technology imports, and, most essential, arrangements for fostering innovation and diffusion. Without attention to these aspects, additional spending on R and D may be largely wasted.

FUNDAMENTAL RESEARCH

It has sometimes been noted that LDCs tend to favour fundamental rather than applied research. In Venezuela, for example, it was estimated that in 1963, 74 per cent of the research was fundamental, 22 per cent applied and only 4 per cent development,[1] while in Mexico almost all the research was aimed at increasing basic knowledge.[2] By contrast, fundamental research accounts for less than 20 per cent, sometimes less than 10 per cent of total R and D in most industrialized countries.

In part this may be attributable to the relatively high contribution which universities make to the total research effort in many LDCs. Fundamental research is generally accepted as an essential part of a vital science teaching faculty at post-graduate level. Research is certainly necessary for training research workers, and to avoid the problems raised by sending nationals for training in developed countries, local post-graduate training facilities on a limited scale may be needed in LDCs. At the undergraduate level, universities not directly involved with research need not necessarily lose touch with scientific advances, so that their teaching becomes out of date, but they will obviously benefit from building up close relationships with research centres.

Fundamental or basic research has been defined as a search for new knowledge, intended not for application to any specific end, but as a contribution to the conceptual development of our

[1] UNESCO: *La politica cientifica en America Latina*. Science policy study No. 14, p. 14, Paris, 1969.
[2] Victor Urquidi: op. cit.

understanding of nature. Applied research, on the other hand, is defined as a search for a new knowledge with the aim of solving a pre-determined problem. In practice the boundaries are often nebulous, and the distinctions may exist more in the eye of the beholder than in reality. Within fundamental research a similar distinction can be made between free or 'pure' research, as a disinterested search for greater understanding, and oriented basic research, which is directed to a particular field with evident relation to areas of social or economic interest. A great deal of current fundamental research, as for example that financed through the U.S. space programme, or most of the basic research carried out within industry, falls in this latter category.

Fundamental research, therefore, is not necessarily without economic motivation, though the financial returns may be uncertain and, most probably, in the relatively far distant future. But no satisfactory criteria have been found for measuring the economic value of any particular piece of fundamental research, and the choice of what is likely to prove fruitful must rest to a considerable extent on the scientist himself.

Scientists often show a preference for 'pure' research. In part this may be because fundamental research which is unrelated to the practical problems of the outside world is, as a direct consequence, easier to get started and less subject to external constraints. But there may be other valid reasons. Totally un-directed research has been described as science's oldest and noblest mission,[1] and for some, advancing the frontiers of knowledge is a sufficient end in itself. 'Pure' science is regarded as an activity of essentially cultural or intellectual value, beyond the constraints of national boundaries, and the scientists in-volved regard themselves as members of an international *élite*. This can easily lead to an attitude of intellectual snobbishness, whereby applied research is despised as inferior, though in practice it can be as challenging intellectually as fundamental research.

But significant advances in 'pure' research are made only by those few first-class minds with a special aptitude and interest in such research. Except perhaps in areas of 'big science',

[1] UNESCO: *Science policy and the European States.* Conference of Ministers of the European Member States Responsible for Science Policy, Paris, 1970.

which involve heavy capital outlays, for these rare individuals a substantial measure of freedom to pursue their own interests, without regard to tangible economic benefits, may be warranted. This may lead not only to individual achievement, but may contribute to national prestige and esteem. A Nobel Prize may be comparable in satisfaction to an Olympic Gold Medal, though neither may increase the standard of living.

However, for the majority of researchers, satisfaction can be found equally well in oriented basic research or in applied research. In LDCs the primary emphasis needs to be on applied research, and such oriented fundamental research as is required to support the applied research programme. While full advantage should be taken of fundamental work carried out elsewhere, some local fundamental research may be necessary to maintain contact with, and an understanding of, important relevant work in other countries—it has been described as a window on the world of science. The results of fundamental research may be universally available, but someone must be able to speak the language.

In some cases the basic knowledge required may not be available, and fundamental research will have to be carried out locally. This may well be necessary, for example, in studies on the environment, or on natural resources. Primarily, this fundamental research should be related, however tenuously, with research lines which are relevant to development or which will be relevant in the future, and which are likely to be most useful in the generation of indigenous technologies. Basic research can thus contribute to development, but the expenditure involved is likely to be kept at a relatively low proportion of the total research effort.

Excessive priority towards either science for its own sake or science as a servant of economic growth should be avoided. Neither extreme can exist alone, and science policy must be concerned with ensuring a proper balance between the two, with mutual interaction and inter-communication. Some scientists often object to the concept of science planning as inimical to academic freedom and the autonomy of the university research worker. But planning is essentially concerned with broad issues of policies and priorities, and not the detailed control of individual research projects of interference with the initiative of the university research worker. Over-emphasis of scientific freedom, on the other hand, often leads to wasted efforts.

REGIONAL CO-OPERATION

The limited human and financial resources for science and technology in developing countries clearly suggest the value of co-operation between countries, particularly in the field of agriculture between countries sharing the same ecological region. But such co-operation can be expected to succeed only to the extent that national policies and programmes have first been defined to suit each country's needs and development goals, and the results can be implemented by national organiza-tions. As pointed out at the Lagos Conference,[1] a policy regarding resources—much more complex a matter than re-search on resources—is one of the essential political and economic prerogatives of governments, which must each determine its own strategy.

In practice, there is little sign of any increase in regional co-operation. The West African and Central African research centres, for example, have been disbanded, and there is some uncertainty about the future of East African research. Though considerable successes have been achieved by some inter-national centres, notably the agricultural centres initiated by the Ford and Rockefeller Foundations, as discussed further in a later section, it seems wise to accept as a fact the national desires of each country to have its own research organization, which will in any case promote contact between research and its application, and to encourage governments to allow their scientists the means of communicating effectively with their colleagues in neighbouring countries. A realistic approach would suggest that science policies, particularly in relation to industrialization and the commercial exploitation of natural resources, should be directed towards the strengthening of national institutions and infrastructures.

---

[1] UNESCO/ECA: *Final report of the Lagos Conference.* Paris, 1964, p. 36.

III Agricultural Development

INTRODUCTION

The potential impact of technological change on agricultural development has been dramatically demonstrated in the last few years by the so-called 'Green Revolution' in cereal production. Improved varieties of wheat, rice, and other cereals, developed through sophisticated biological engineering techniques, and grown in association with an array of modernized agricultural practices, have allowed significant increases in outputs. The widespread acceptance of these new technologies in Asia, rising from 200 acres in 1965 to 34,000,000 acres in 1969,[1] has for a while at least transformed the food supply situation. This development has brought Pakistan from being the second largest recipient of U.S. food aid in 1967 to the brink of cereal self-sufficiency. Assuming political stability, India may be able to feed her population from her own resources by the mid-1970s. While the new seeds have had the greatest impact in Asia and in Mexico, other countries, notably Kenya and the Ivory Coast, have also made important gains from an agricultural base.

Throughout the course of history, agriculture has broadly kept up with population increases, partly through the cultivation of more land, and partly through improved technology. In recent decades, with the very rapid rate of population growth in most LDCs, food production has barely kept pace, and in some countries has fallen behind. LDCs have moved from being net exporters of cereals in the 1930s to net importers in the 1960s. It has been estimated that 'Even in a good year their imports of food from the developed world comes to about $4 billion, a serious and unnecessary drain on their balance of payments with the developed world.'[2] Generally,

---

[1] Lester R. Brown: *Seeds of change, The Green Revolution and development in the 1970s.* Praeger, 1970, p. 4.

[2] W. A. Lewis: *The development process.* Executive Briefing Paper, No. 2, United Nations Centre for Economic and Social Information, 1970, p. 8.

the situation has not allowed any substantial increase in the *per capita* consumption of basic foods, let alone any significant qualitative rise in nutrition standards. Hence increasing emphasis has been placed on improving food supplies, in both quantity and quality.

In few countries is there much scope for meeting these needs through exploiting virgin lands. The new technological advances in cereal production, however, offer a temporary respite by allowing substantial increases in yields per acre. Yield increases of wheat in India and Pakistan since 1967 have exceeded those of the past several decades.A number of other countries—particularly Turkey, Afghanistan, Tunisia, Morocco, and Iran—appear to be on the verge of similar yield take-offs in wheat.[1] Similar advances, though as yet much less dramatic, are being made with rice. These yield improvements have contributed to the production trends shown in the graph on the facing page.

Not all of the increases can be attributed to improved technology. An analysis of the record production in India and Pakistan in 1968 showed weather as the major single factor, while high-yielding varieties, with associated fertilizers and irrigation water, accounted for 30 per cent of the increase in India, and 15 per cent in West Pakistan.[2] However, the contribution of the new varieties will undoubtedly rise as the proportion of land under them is increased. Possibly even more important are the prospects from multiple cropping, illustrated by the spectacular gains achieved in Taiwan, where land productivity climbed 300 per cent between 1950 and 1965 as farmers both adopted improved rices and planted more crops per acre.[3]

The new technologies could not have been effective in isolation, and probably would have made relatively much less impact a few years earlier, before the necessary infrastructure, particularly improved water supply and roads, had been developed. The introduction of the new seeds happily came immediately after the droughts of 1966/7, which had led

[1] Lester R. Brown: op. cit., p. 38.
[2] D. G. Dalrymple: *Technological change in agriculture. Effects and implications for the developing nations*. Foreign Agricultural Service, U.S.D.A., 1969, p. 42.
[3] Lester R. Brown: op. cit., p. 41.

governments to adopt guaranteed minimum prices, making the use of fertilizers economic. Technology is but one of the many factors which limit agricultural improvement.

Equally, higher yields do not necessarily lead to sustained economic growth. Without further developments, the effects of the new levels of productivity will soon be swamped by population growth. While most countries now accept the vital importance of restraining this growth, control measures are inevitably slow to take effect. Meantime there is the danger

FIGURE 5
WHEAT AND RICE PRODUCTION TRENDS IN SELECTED COUNTRIES, 1960–9

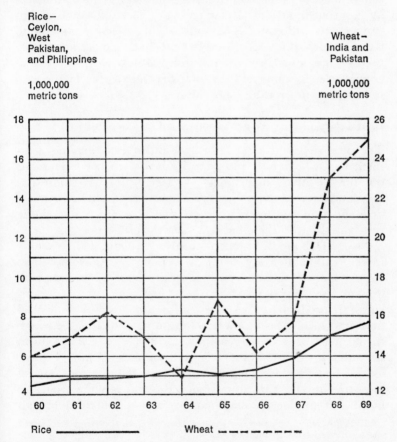

Source: Based on Brown, *Seeds of change.*

that, as in the past, marginal technical advances will merely extend the road to subsistence equilibrium, allowing more people to live at subsistence level on a given area of land. In Java, for example, technical advances in agriculture supported a six-fold increase in population between 1850 and 1961, without significant changes in living conditions, and with little structural transformation. But over the same period, similar advances in traditional labour-intensive agriculture in Japan 'came to be complementarily related to an expanding manufacturing system in indigenous hands', and it was 'the dynamic interaction between the two sectors which kept Japan moving and ultimately pushed her over the hump to sustained growth'.[1] Without such structural change, the effects of technical improvements will soon be dissipated. The objective must be to see that output increases from technical change are not simply used up by an increasing population, but lead to the growth of commercial farming and an inter-dependent development of industry, commerce, and agriculture.

INDUSTRIAL AND AGRICULTURAL INTER-DEPENDENCE

The inter-dependence of industrial and agricultural development is now generally recognized. Over-simplified arguments on the relative importance of agricultural or industrial development have given way to a concept of concurrent growth, depending on a technically progressive agriculture, interacting substantially with the other sectors of the economy.

Most LDCs are still predominantly rural, and with available investment capital are likely to remain so for some time. Employment in industry will increase slowly, but industrial growth itself depends on markets. Equally, improved agricultural productivity requires a greater use of industrial products, such as fertilizers or water pumps, to purchase which the farmer must have increased off-farm sales. The agricultural sector has a vital role not merely as a source of labour and cheap food to be tapped by the industrial sector, but as a consumer of industrial products, a supplier of industrial raw materials, an avenue of productive employment, and a source of foreign

[1] B. F. Johnston: *Agriculture and economic development: the relevance of the Japanese experience*. Food Research Institute Studies, Stanford University, VI, No. 3, 1966, p. 283.

exchange earnings, and ultimately of investment capital. In Japan, for example, over the period 1895 to 1960, through land tax and other mechanisms, agriculture was able to provide a considerable net contribution to capital formation for the rest of the economy.[1]

Recognition of this inter-dependence does not of course make agricultural development any easier. The comparative neglect of agriculture by some LDC governments may be due less to lack of interest than to a recognition of the complex problems involved. Agricultural development requires the effective exploitation of modern technologies by many millions of people, with concomitant changes in attitudes and institutions, and extensive investment in organization and infrastructure. According to an FAO study

the countries of Latin America that have been the most successful in achieving balanced development of agriculture and industry have been those that have planned and expended in the agricultural sector much more energy and effort and public investments than they have in the industrial sector. This proportion is not un-economic, however. In the long run, the costs of agricultural development have proved to be investments that are repaying themselves many times. But, most importantly, these costs must be supported, because industry has not been able to progress beyond a certain rudimentary stage unless agriculture has been helped to make great strides forward.[2]

Where agriculture accounts for a significant part of the GNP, evidently overall growth will be considerably dependent on growth in the agricultural sector. A sustained growth of over 5 per cent in this sector is rare, and Chenery has noted that 'the Ivory Coast appears to be the only country that has sustained a 6 per cent rate of growth for as much as a decade starting with an agricultural sector of more than 50 per cent GNP'.[3] As the share of industry in total output rises, however, the growth potential rises. From an analysis of structural changes in a

[1] B. F. Johnston and J. Cownie: *The seed-fertiliser revolution and labour force absorption*. American Economic Review, Sept., 1969.

[2] C. Mitchell and J. Schatan: 'The outlook for agricultural development in Latin America'. In *Agricultural development in Latin America in the next decade*. Inter-American Development Bank, 1967, p. 88.

[3] H. Chenery: 'Targets for development'. Columbia University Conference on International Economic Development, 1970, p. 7.

number of countries, Chenery concluded that, 'although an increase in accumulation and other conditions are required to achieve this result, enough countries have been able to accelerate growth in this way so that it may be regarded as a norm for a well functioning economy in the income range of $100–$400— provided foreign assistance is available in the early stages.'

AGRICULTURAL DEVELOPMENT

In many countries, agricultural development is still greatly neglected. Arthur Lewis has observed that 'if one were asked to pick a single factor as the most common cause of a low rate of economic growth it would have to be the absence of a vigorous agricultural policy'. 'Agricultural stagnation is the main constraint on the rate of growth.'[1]

The FAO Survey[2] in Latin America, for example, has noted that agriculture is not properly fulfilling its important role in development. It does not furnish the foods necessary for a good diet for Latin Americans, nor the exports necessary to provide foreign exchange for the developing nations. Much of the land is wasted through lack of proper husbandry, while human resources are wasted because millions of farm people are not given the opportunity of improving their farming ability and their incomes. 'This severe judgement on the status of agriculture in Latin America must be laid at the doorstep of the governments, the business enterprises, the banks, public and private, and the land owners of the region more than on the farmers themselves.'

The low status of agriculture is evidenced by the very low yield levels. Yields from livestock, for example, whether per head or per acre, are far lower than the world average in all countries of Latin America except Argentina, Uruguay and Chile. One of the strongest obstacles to increased production and productivity lies in the feudal system of land tenure, which has left the ownership of at least three-quarters of the agricultural lands of Latin America in the hands of those who own only 15 per cent of the total number of farms. Concentration of ownership has not necessarily produced the best results. In one

[1] W. A. Lewis: *Development planning.* Allen & Unwin, 1966, p. 270.
[2] C. Mitchell and J. Schatan: op. cit., p. 45.

large Latin American country, farmers on family-sized enterprises produced an output valued at 880 monetary units per hectare, while the large owners had a gross output of only 170 of the same monetary units per hectare.[1] Other major problems are lack of credit, extension facilities, and organized markets.

In general, agricultural development may be limited by many factors and a systems approach is essential. Mosher, for example, has identified ten factors as being universal for agricultural development, of which five are 'essentials', including markets, technology, local availability of input supplies, production incentives, and transportation. Without any one of these there can be no agricultural development. In addition there are 'accelerators' to development, which are important but not indispensable, including education, production credit, group action by farmers, land improvement and development, and national planning. [2]

Due attention needs therefore to be given to every aspect— improved technologies, farm supplies and services, incentives, transport and storage, markets, credit—and the critical limiting factor or factors identified in each case. The solution of technical problems is but one link in the chain, and may itself create new problems. As results are extended to farmers, demand will rise for manufactured inputs, for storage and marketing facilities, and for capital, without which improved technology may be largely useless.

AGRICULTURAL STRATEGY

For most countries the ultimate aim of agricultural development is likely to be a fully commercial agriculture, with a high level of sophistication and a very limited subsistence element, but the strategic emphasis will depend on the specific circumstances, which may vary greatly from one area to another within any one country. Hunter[3] has observed that agricultural

[1] Ibid., p. 52.

[2] A. T. Mosher: *Getting agriculture moving. Essentials for development and modernisation.* Agricultural Development Council. Praeger, 1966, p. 61. Also discussed in *Asian agricultural survey.* Asian Development Bank, University of Tokyo Press, 1969, p. 239.

[3] G. Hunter: *Modernizing peasant societies. A comparative study in Asia and Africa.* Oxford University Press, 1969, p. 83.

policies are often described in terms of objectives, of which the most important are probably the improvement of total food supplies and qualitatively, of nutrition; a substantial rise in farmers' incomes, largely by the development of a full market economy; a growth and diversification of employment. These objectives are not necessarily consistent, and the particular policy to be followed in any area will be a product of the inter-action of relative priorities and the specific ecological environ-ment, taking a localized rather than a national view.

One of the most decisive factors affecting development strategy is population growth. At any conceivable rate of industrialization, the rural population will continue to increase in most countries for many years. For example, in West Pakistan, even assuming that the increase in non-farm employ-ment were to continue at its recent high rate of 4·5 per cent per annum, the farm labour force would increase from 7·4 M. in 1961 to 12·2 M. in 1985.[1] For most African countries, with some 80 per cent of the population in rural areas, the 0–21 age group accounts for over 60 per cent of the total population. Without a significant reduction in the population growth rate or a phenomenal rise in productive urban employment, these societies will remain agrarian for a very long time.

A substantial increase in the rural labour force is therefore to be anticipated in most LDCs. The strategy of agricultural development will largely determine a country's ability to absorb this growing labour force into productive employment. This raises a crucial issue which has been described as a choice between the 'Japanese model' and the 'Mexican model', the contrasting features of which have been analysed by Johnston.[2]

In essence, the contrast between the Japanese and Mexican approaches to agricultural development lies in the fact that the increase in farm output and productivity in Japan resulted from the widespread adoption of improved techniques by the great majority of the nation's farmers, whereas in Mexico the major part of the impressive increases in agricultural output in the post-war period has been the result of substantial increases in production by a very small number of large-scale, highly commercial farm operators.

[1] B. F. Johnston and J. Cownie: op. cit., p. 16.
[2] B. F. Johnston: op. cit., p. 285.

The Mexican approach was successful in exploiting the opportunities which became available for rapid and profitable expansion of cotton and wheat. But the bulk of the country's farmers were largely by-passed, and while many may eventually be absorbed into non-farm employment the Mexican economy is now composed of a comparatively well-to-do minority in industry or in commercial agriculture, and a semi-subsistence majority.

Japan's experience demonstrates the potential that exists for increasing farm output within the framework of a small-scale labour-intensive agriculture by the development and widespread adoption of yield-increasing innovations.

For many LDCs it is even more important today than during the early period of development in Japan to emphasize the type of agricultural development strategy that is suggested by the 'Japanese model'. This implies creating the conditions necessary for expanding farm output by making available new inputs such as improved varieties, fertilizers, and irrigation water, improved implements useful for breaking seasonal bottlenecks and improved technical knowledge—but all designed primarily to complement and make more effective use of the labour resources which are and for some time are likely to remain relatively abundant in most LDCs. Obversely, achieving increases in farm output and productivity by a heavy reliance on the use of scarce resources of capital and foreign exchange to purchase equipment which is mainly labour-saving should be avoided.

But as Johnston points out

although the broad strategy underlying Japan's approach to agricultural development seems to have considerable relevance to many contemporary underdeveloped countries, it certainly does not follow that the techniques that were used to increase farm productivity and output in Japan can merely be copied. In fact, one of the principal lessons to be derived from the Japanese experience is the importance of progressively modifying existing farming systems rather than attempting the wholesale substitution of 'modern' for 'traditional' agriculture.[1]

In practice, many countries have tended towards capital-intensive development, based on mechanization and intensive

[1] Ibid., p. 287.

settlement schemes, often with indifferent results despite heavy expenditure of scarce resources concentrated on a very limited section of the population. To some extent, this tendency may be attributed to an identification of modernization with mechanization, while scorning traditional agriculture as primitive—a view reinforced by and contributing to discrepancies between private and social returns on investment in labour-saving equipment.

The new technologies in cereal production are relevant to both large-scale and small-scale farming, but larger farmers have readier access to the capital needed to develop water supplies, and have less difficulties in buying fertilizers or selling their crops at the best prices. On these larger holdings, as for example in West Pakistan, where production improvements have been concentrated among 10 per cent of the bigger farmers operating 40 per cent of the land area,[1] often the bullock is regarded as obsolete, and the seed-fertilizer revolution may encourage premature tractor mechanization—probably uneconomic from the society's point of view, even if profitable to large farm operators.[2] There is some danger that the net effect will be increased social inequalities, and a considerable rise in rural unemployment. This trend may be encouraged by a too rapid increase in labour costs. Already in Northern India and West Pakistan, seasonal labour shortages have forced rural wages during harvest to rise above the normal city level.

But modern technologies also offer possibilities for increased employment, particularly through multiple cropping. On a given plot of land, two, three or sometimes even four crops per year are becoming feasible, leading to significant increases in farm labour requirements. In Taiwan, for example, where multiple cropping has been widely adopted (see p. 81), working days required per acre per annum have doubled. In West Pakistan farmers found that increased cropping intensity was associated with a substantial increase in the rate of use of the existing farm labour force and bullock power.[3]

If agriculture is to make its due contribution to reducing

[1] L. S. Hardin: 'Later generation agricultural development problems'. Conference on agricultural development, Bellagio, 1969, p. 7.
[2] B. F. Johnston and J. Cownie: op. cit., p. 13.
[3] Ibid., p. 9.

poverty, agricultural systems are needed which can make full use of the rural labour force, while offering maximum returns. Long-term economic growth, as well as the welfare of the rural majority who will necessarily remain in agriculture for some time, may depend on an agricultural development strategy directed at raising the productivity of the existing small-scale, labour-intensive agriculture.

The danger of increased inequalities applies not only within a locality, but also between localities. The recent technological advances have been primarily concerned with irrigated cereal crops. These can become extremely profitable, in comparison with other crops, particularly with high support prices. According to an Asian Regional Study,[1] the lower production costs resulting from the use of the new technology should enable farmers to produce cereals profitably at reduced prices, even allowing a somewhat higher profit factor to cover risks associated with the much higher levels of cash inputs required for modern farming. But reduced prices would immediately increase the problems in the non-irrigated low rainfall areas, where there is little chance of using fertilizers profitably.

The FAO World Plan for Agricultural Development[2] advocates a low-cost approach to raising productivity in these areas, with particular emphasis on introducing leguminous fodder crops into rotation with cereals, so as to allow a closer integration of crop and livestock production, with increased employment, and also to raise yields through providing nitrogen and animal manure.

The full benefits of intensified agriculture in irrigated areas and improved basic food supplies, may come only with increased specialization into other food crops and into raw materials for agro-based industries, including the extensive development of livestock and forestry, in appropriate areas.

IMPROVED TECHNOLOGY

In the past it has sometimes been assumed that technology was not a limiting factor in improving tropical agriculture. It was

---

[1] FAO: *Provisional indicative world plan for agricultural development—summary and main conclusions.* Rome, 1970, p. 33.

[2] Ibid., p. 51.

6

thought that adequate technical knowledge was already available and that the primary need was improved extension to bring this knowledge to the farmers. When the International Rice Research Institute was first mooted, for example, it was opposed on the ground that the major problem was to get the available information to the farmers through improved or re-organized extension services. Education, transportation, marketing systems, and industrialization were considered more important than agricultural research.[1] But earlier attempts to raise rice yields in South-East Asia by extension of Japanese methods failed through lack of proper varieties and practices. Initial rice experiments at IRRI were wiped out by borer, virus, and blast, and development of the new varieties required a considerable team effort involving plant breeders, geneticists, plant pathologists, organic chemists, agronomists, and engineers.[2]

At the centre of the agricultural revolution lie varieties which can effectively exploit high fertility conditions, derived from the use of fertilizers and improved water supply. More generally, the technical aspects of modern farming are concerned with the management and use of the environment to produce economically useful organisms which have to be protected against harmful competition or damage by harmful organisms.[3] Success requires a complete package of technology adapted to local conditions, including appropriate fertilizer-use techniques, adequate means of pest and disease control, together with necessary planting, cultivation, and irrigation techniques. In the case of animals the package may include proper strains, nutrition techniques, and management. To be effective, nothing important can be left out.[4]

Agricultural technology must be tailored to suit the specific conditions of each farming area, with its unique combination of soil factors, moisture, day length, temperature, pest and disease complex, and human preferences. Account must be taken too of the economic, social, and physical aspects of the environment which condition the feasibility of new techniques.

[1] S. Wortman: *The crop production equation*. Weed Society of America, 1967, p. 8.
[2] S. Wortman: *The technological basis for intensified agriculture*. Rockefeller Foundation, 1969, p. 30.
[3] A. H. Bunting (ed.): *Change in Agriculture*. Duckworth, London, 1970, p. 728.
[4] S. Wortman: op. cit., p. 20.

Hence, while basic scientific knowledge, and sometimes the practical results of applied research, can be usefully transferred from a temperate to a tropical country without loss of validity, much of the development of agricultural technology must necessarily be done in the area under local conditions.[1]

Though there have been considerable advances, these represent but a start towards solving the massive problems of tropical food and industrial crops and agricultural systems. Until the recent developments in cereals, research effort in tropical food crops was relatively limited and the strongest evidence of the potential which technological improvements could offer related to export crops. The commodity research institute approach has been fairly general, and striking results have been achieved in rubber, cocoa, and many other export crops.

But though individual research stations have often done much useful work, piecemeal innovation in a particular crop has its limitations. Research may have been applied to a specific crop, without taking rotations, or the problems of mixed farming, into full account. Frequently insufficient attention has been paid to the economic aspects or to overall farm management problems to make innovations feasible. Ultimately, the success of research is measured by the impact on a country's agricultural output. This depends on research which is not only competent, but is based on a sound knowledge of local farming systems and an understanding of the farmers' problems and attitudes. Comprehensive studies of the economics of innovation are needed, with sufficient trials to test and demonstrate the practicality of results at the farm level.[2] In sum, 'Effective research systems begin with problem solving at central research stations and do not end until a complete package of practices is available for the ultimate site—the individual farm.'[3]

In general, past failures have often been due to the incompleteness or unprofitability of recommended technologies, or to the farmers' inability to take advantage of useful technology because inputs, such as fertilizers, were not available, prices unfavourable, or markets inaccessible. When farmers fail to

[1] Ibid., p. 20.

[2] J. C. de Wilde et al: Experience with agricultural development in tropical Africa. The synthesis. John Hopkins Press, 1967, p. 39.

[3] S. Wortman: Meeting protein needs through plant breeding. Getting the job done. Rockefeller Foundation, p. 12.

adopt innovations, the fault may well lie with the scientists, economists, national leaders, or private industry. The evidence suggests that the farmer is willing, often eager, to change if offered a substantial profit.

AGRICULTURAL RESEARCH

Agricultural research involves the application of the basic principles of a wide range of scientific disciplines to the solution of problems of both immediate and prospective significance to agriculture. This implies, on the one hand, a broad fundamental research support, including access to international sources of information and materials, and, on the other hand, an organization able to apply scientific knowledge to practical problems, and to translate the results into working methods acceptable to farmers. While many problems in tropical agriculture can be solved through the application of existing scientific knowledge, it must be remembered that this has been derived mainly in temperate climates. Basic research may therefore be required to solve problems of local significance or to exploit local resources, quite apart from its value in maintaining contact with useful scientific and technological developments elsewhere. To concentrate solely on applied research would be a short-sighted policy, and a proper balance between basic and applied research is important.

It is equally important to maintain a balance between short-term problem solving and long-term objectives. In a comprehensive study of the organization and administration of agricultural research, Arnon[1] has observed that within the same framework an efficient agricultural research organization can comprise two basically different types of research units, whose goals are apt to be divergent: those based on scientific disciplines, whose major and probably overriding concern is to further knowledge, each in his own field, thus tending to foster narrow interests; and those based on fields of production, whose aim and responsibility is to further knowledge which is directly related to improving production, in their respective fields, whether by increasing yields, improving quality, or creating

[1] I. Arnon: *Organisation and administration of agricultural research*. Elsevier, 1968, p. 147.

new uses, which exhibit a tendency to neglect basic research in favour of empirical studies. The goals of the 'production' departments cannot be achieved without harnessing the full potentialities offered by the 'discipline' departments, and providing for the maximum integration of their efforts.

The need to sustain long-term objectives against pressures of short-term expediency also suggests the value of a research organization having some degree of autonomy. It has been affirmed[1] that their relative independence from political, opportunist, and other short-term pressures has been a large part of the secret of the success of the research programmes of the Ford and Rockefeller Foundations, the French overseas research organizations, and commercially-supported commodity research stations.

Apart from technical aspects, attention needs to be paid to farm economics and to the practicability and social implications of proposed innovations. To this end agricultural economists, practical agriculturists and social anthropologists should be intimately associated with the planning, execution, and evaluation of research work, and the research stations themselves should engage in pilot testing of research results in the farmers' milieu.[2] There is often a lack of appreciation of the scope and depth which is needed in research systems, and particularly of the importance of local farm testing. Some research establishments do not recognize this as within their responsibility or interest—an attitude which is not conducive to a profitable return on research investment.

The effectiveness of an agricultural research organization depends very largely on building up a communications system between the various research workers, and also between research workers, extension workers and the farmers. To make a useful contribution to agricultural development, an institutional structure is required which links together farm problems, local adaptive research, centralized basic research and international scientific resources. A national agricultural research system therefore comprises inter-disciplinary research at central experimental stations, with experimentation and testing at centres in each farming region, through to further testing and

---

[1] A. H. Bunting: op. cit., p. 740.
[2] J. C. de Wilde: op. cit., p. 234.

demonstration on farms in each locality. All personnel, from research scientists to extension workers, are essentially part of a single system, and must be integrated into a co-ordinated team.

The characteristics of such a system have been summarized in the conclusions of an International Seminar on Change in Agriculture held at the University of Reading in 1968.

All experience confirms that agricultural progress ideally requires stable, continuing, authoritative institutions, staffed by a permanent or at least long-term staff of capable and experienced workers, whose programmes of work are competently and consistently directed to solve important practical problems, and whose results are transferred with their help and in a practical form to those who have to use them.[1]

But few LDCs are equipped with such a broadly integrated system. More typically they suffer from poor research organization, with weak leadership and co-ordination, inadequate facilities, limited and usually short-term allocations of funds, and a chronic shortage of agricultural scientists. Organizational weaknesses may lead to frequent and continual transfers of subordinate level research workers from one project to another, for the sake of modest salary advances, with the result that they can make little contribution to advancing technology. 'The lack of nationally structured research organisations together with inadequate numbers of well-trained research specialists have been the more critical limitations in generating agricultural technology in the developing countries.'[2]

In Africa, former British colonies typically have a central research institute concerned mainly with fundamental research related to cash or export crops, but limited attention is paid to broad-scale adaptive research. Inter-linked specialized research institutes in French-speaking African countries have important advantages in personnel and focus, but again there are few general agricultural stations to relate specialized institutes to the farm problems as a whole. As a result, the basic weakness seems to be a lack of well-derived and tested improvements which are seen by the farmers as clearly rewarding. By exem-

[1] A. H. Bunting: op. cit., p. 740.
[2] A. H. Moseman: 'Building agricultural research systems in the developing nations'. Monograph of the Agricultural Development Council, New York, 1970, p. 64.

plary contrast, de Wilde[1] attributes the success of a programme in Bouaké, Ivory Coast, as due in considerable part to advance testing of a package of new practices on a pilot scale and to the effective collaboration of a general agricultural research station and a specialized cotton research institution in developing an effective way of introducing a profitable cotton crop without upsetting the existing farming system.

The Asian Development Bank Agricultural Survey identifies three major constraints on research:

1. a grave shortage of highly trained technical manpower;
2. insufficient funds and other supports from governments, mostly a national budget problem but probably also arising from a low expectancy for research results;
3. lack of an effective system for co-ordinating research activities with extension services, sometimes further aggravated by organizational weakness within research centres themselves which usually results in wasteful overlapping and dilution of efforts.[2]

Evidently it takes time to build up an effective organization which covers all the essential fields, with the minimum of duplication. But while lack of technical and administrative personnel may dictate a limited scale of operations initially, a basic organizational blueprint can be useful as a framework for development, and as a guide to making the best use of technical assistance.

On funds, the Survey Report comments that

domestic finance for additional research seems to be the most difficult element in the agricultural development process to obtain, and among the most difficult to find support from external aid sources as well. Yet, it is acknowledged that it is from research that the leverage for development came in the form of new high yielding, responsive varieties, and that it will be from research that the capability of sustaining development will come.[3]

Some indications of the range of variation in expenditure on agricultural research may be seen in the following table though there have been marked improvements in recent years.

[1] J. C. de Wilde: op. cit., p. 36.
[2] *Asian agricultural survey*: op. cit., p. 246.
[3] Ibid., p. 77.

TABLE 2
GOVERNMENT RESEARCH BUDGETS

Country	Year	Cost per farmer	Research budgets (US $1,000)
Taiwan	1960	$0·49	735
India	1960	0·05	6,843
Japan	1960	0·69	12,558
Philippines	1960	0·27	1,545
Thailand	1960	0·05	564
Mexico	1962	0·35	2,100
United States	1961	45·90	250,000

Source: *Agricultural Development*, USDA, September 1967/No. 35.

The evidence suggests that investment in appropriate agricultural research can offer high returns. Griliches has assessed the return on U.S. research leading to hybrid corn at 700 per cent per annum, while Ewell estimated that for the economy as a whole the U.S. had achieved a return of 100–200 per cent per annum per dollar spent on agricultural R and D over 1937–51.[1] The total expenditure at the International Rice Research Institute (IRRI), including the initial investment in 1962 and subsequent year-to-year operating costs, was $15 million in 1968, while Sterling Wortman of the Rockefeller Foundation estimated that the 1967/8 rice harvest in Asia was $300 million higher because of the new IRRI varieties, and possibly a billion dollars higher for 1968/9. Deducting the additional production costs associated with the new varieties would still leave an exceedingly high return on the original investment.[2]

But elsewhere Wortman[3] observes that much of the world's present agricultural research is probably not profitable. It is often carried out by poorly trained people, or without adequate support, or lacking concern with urgent needs. In these circumstances, research may be a useless economic burden.

In the early stages of development, agricultural research, and equally extension, are of necessity in the main public sector activities. But as intensification increases, the private sector can

[1] Z. Griliches: 'Research costs and social returns: hybrid corn and related innovations'. *Journal of Political Economy*, LXVI, No. 5, 1958, p. 428.
[2] Lester R. Brown: op. cit., p. 49.
[3] S. Wortman: *The technological basis for intensified agriculture*. Rockefeller Foundation, 1969, p. 23.

play an increasingly useful role. In the U.S. in 1965, agri-business research financed by industry accounted for 54 per cent of total agricultural research expenditure. In some LDCs, private companies, including multinational corporations, are now becoming important in supply and service functions, particularly in Asia. Processing industries too may ultimately make significant research contributions.

EXTENSION SERVICES

Extension services provide the two-way link connecting farmers to technical know-how and research. The extension worker has not only to encourage farmers to adopt improved methods, but must represent the farmers' problems and needs to the research workers. In fulfilling these roles, the approaches and methods used must be tailored to suit the particular circumstances and the degree of development of the local community.

The immediate problems may not demand research or improved technology. The key may be investment, often on quite a small scale—for better water supply, storage facilities, fencing for grazing, or farm buildings. But significant improvements are likely to require new techniques, most of which will require new inputs which the farmer will need to buy, using the proceeds from the additional produce he will have to sell. There is no point in expending substantial resources to promote these new techniques unless adequate attention is given to the other constraints, such as markets and credit facilities. Given a strong extension service, with something worthwhile to offer, and attention to these other limiting factors, then agricultural change can be rapid—but all these ingredients must be present if the effort is to be successful.

A technical solution to a particular problem developed at a central research station does not necessarily constitute 'something worthwhile to offer'. Research workers often have a strong technical bias, and tend to over-simplify or may in fact be unaware of the complexities of the farmers' problems. Before they can be useful, the research results must be fully adapted to suit local conditions, and integrated into the farming system. The farmer must be presented with new methods through which he can gain significant benefits by means which are accessible to him. Frequently ignored are the risks involved. A small farmer just cannot afford to spend money on fertilizers unless he is virtually certain of having his money back.

Extension services are often deficient in consideration of farm problems as a whole, and may sometimes lack an understanding of indigenous farming patterns, and pay inadequate attention to the impact of particular innovations on these patterns. According to de Wilde,[1] for example, agricultural development failures are largely traceable to inadequate knowledge or insufficient appreciation of the relevance of all the socio-economic factors that determine a proper approach to the farmer and condition his response and receptivity to change.

Peasant societies offer an immense range of variety, but several attempts at classification have been made. Directly relevant to extension problems is that of Hunter,[2] who identifies three broad 'stages' in the continuous process of development. His starting point is the traditional, semi-subsistence rural society (Stage I), where the main emphases are on security and suspicion of the outsider, followed by a transitional phase (Stage II) in which there is already considerable contact and some innovation and cash-cropping, but where the traditional structure of society is still felt to be a necessary support and protection. Individuals will take risks, if the money rewards are tempting, but they will not be willing to challenge the traditional order—the chief, lineage, landlord—directly. Stage III represents a full acceptance of the market system, and the aim of maximizing income by cash farming. There is more individualism; traditional restraints are seen as barriers—there may be a direct challenge to the old leadership. Farming becomes far more sophisticated and technical.

Clearly, different approaches are needed for each stage. Stage I is the classical opportunity for the village-based 'community development' programme, where the trust of villagers may be gained by meeting a non-agricultural need. A big corps of very simply trained staff is needed. At the opposite extreme, in Stage III, community development is 'old hat'—the village is earning more and prefers to

[1] J. C. de Wilde: op. cit., p. 45.
[2] G. Hunter: 'Agricultural change and social development'. Plenary lecture, International Seminar on Change in Agriculture, 1968. In A. H. Bunting: op. cit., p. 26 et seq.

spend its money on its own. Simply trained extension staff are by now useless as advisers (the farmer knows more than they do), though perhaps useful as employees. The extension service needs more competent and specialised personnel, to deal with sophisticated problems of agronomy or disease. . . .

This concept of stages, rough and ill-defined as it is, at least disposes of the universal recipes which used to be common—'the right policy is . . . (community development or graduate extension officers, increased prices, etc.)'. Policy is 'right' only in its local relation.

In modernizing traditional agriculture, Hunter has emphasized the importance of the element of time and sequence—the process of change.

Either in technical or social ways, a single change almost always has multiple effects. . . . The very fact that all aspects of life are interrelated can be regarded as a benefit, because a single acceptable change can work its way through the system, causing other small changes in an impersonal way . . . a single change makes possible two or three subsequent changes, and this process can proceed geometrically; the crunch will come only when the sum of small changes finally comes directly face to face with a major institution of interest. . . .

Sometimes a social change will start the technical process. . . . But more often a technical change, which appears socially innocent, will be easier. It is for this reason, and because *some* resistance is always involved, that we have come to realise that a thoroughly sound and tested technical change which makes a major difference to income . . . is absolutely essential in many cases: the first push must be strong enough to break one link in the circle; thereafter multiple consequences begin to flow.

The sequence in which proven innovations are introduced into a particular farming system may be critical if a cumulative impact is to result. A study by the Food Research Institute of Stanford University[1] has suggested that the appropriateness of different types of innovations and the readiness with which they will be adopted are related to the phase of development as it affects economic feasibility and prevalent socio-psychological attitudes. The traits associated with individual innovations will

[1] *Economic, cultural and technical determinants of agricultural change in tropical Africa.* Food Research Institute, Stanford University, 1969. Preliminary Report No. 2, p. 74.

affect their acceptability. Although the rate of adoption of new techniques and innovations is governed largely by economic feasibility at the farm level, one of the major contributions which technical change makes to early stage agricultural development lies in reducing some of the risks which the farmer is called upon to bear. The lower the risk involved and the more profitable an innovation, the more acceptable it becomes. The criteria of 'reversibility' and 'divisibility' may also be critical. Reversibility refers to the extent to which a major factor such as land can be reverted or restored to the *status quo ante* if the innovation proves uneconomic. The criterion of divisibility refers to the extent to which an innovation such as a new cash crop or farm input can be adopted in small units.[1]

These principles are illustrated by the successful agricultural developments in the Kisii highlands of Kenya.[2] Pyrethrum was introduced into the area in 1952, and by 1959 some 11,500 farmers were producing about $180,000 worth of pyrethrum flower annually. Pyrethrum has the advantage of low risk, because the initial investment is small, and high profitability. Furthermore it is fairly easily reversible and is quite divisible, in that it can be tried out by the farmers at first on a small scale, and in the event of failure the land can be put to an alternative use without too much difficulty. The crop proved so profitable that by the time tea was introduced in 1957, farmers had amassed sufficient 'risk capital' to allow investment in this new crop, though it is much less reversible than pyrethrum. Accumulated farm incomes from tea and pyrethrum allowed the adoption of exotic cattle, which were introduced in 1963. The initial investment required for exotic cattle is high, though the risks involved have been substantially reduced by modern technology. Furthermore, a relatively high level of technical competence in management is demanded: rotational grazing, regular purchases of feed concentrates, and regular spraying against ticks. The sequence in which these innovations were introduced played an important part in their acceptance.

Typically, farmers in traditional agriculture cannot be expected to be on the look-out for improvements, and the role of extension agencies must be active, if not aggressive, in reaching out to the farmer, though they must remain guides and

---

[1] Ibid., p. 75.   [2] Ibid., p. 74 *et seq.*

servants, not masters. The extension staff must seek out the farmers and gain their confidence, convince them of potential benefits, and ensure that recommended practices are fully understood. Inadequate communication may do more harm than good, as for example, when fertilizers are issued without adequate explanations, leading to improper use, lack of response, and rejection of extension advice.

It is relatively easy to reach progressive farmers, particularly if they are fairly well-to-do, with large operations, and so can afford to take risks with the prospect of reaping the full benefits. The problem is to reach the large numbers of farmers with small holdings, but given security of tenure, cheap credit, and appropriate technical advice, small farmers may become equally enterprising, as evidenced in Japan and Taiwan. de Wilde has remarked that

the natural environment over much of tropical Africa is not very favourable to the development of remunerative agriculture, and research and experimentation have failed to a large extent in developing practicable and profitable innovations. On the other hand, experience does demonstrate that many Africans, once they emerge from a subsistence economy and have been exposed to the attractions of money income for some time, respond readily to demonstrated profit opportunities.[1]

Experience generally has discredited the earlier view that peasants would not respond to incentives.

In some Latin American countries, where a few substantial commercial farms co-exist with large numbers of small holdings, the research and extension services, and also the institutional arrangements, such as credit facilities, may be heavily biased in favour of the large landowners, who have inevitably tended to dominate agricultural policy. Limited access to secondary education may have meant that few qualified people have come from the poorer agricultural sector, and the social gap between technicians and illiterate peasants may be so great that extension agents prefer to work with large farmers. A complete overhaul of the institutional structure may be essential if the great majority of the rural population is to benefit.

More generally, in many LDCs extension services have to be

[1] J. C. de Wilde: op. cit., p. 64.

manned with personnel of limited education, who have had little or no practical experience in technical farming. Even graduate-level extension officers often do not know how to farm and typically come from the cities or from traditional farms where they will have had no background in practical modern farming. Such personnel are relatively useless in promoting intensive agriculture. The success of IRRI has depended to a great extent on a basic philosophy that an effective extension worker must be able to grow rice at least as well as a farmer, and be able to diagnose his problems and prescribe remedies. IRRI in fact has dropped the term 'extension worker' in favour of 'production specialist', and has developed intensive short-term training programmes to teach these 'change agents' the basic skills and some of the fundamental knowledge of tropical rice production.

Conventional organization of extension may not provide the linkage between research and the farmer that is necessary for success at the farm level. An interesting attempt to strengthen this link may be seen at the Ahmadu Bello University in Northern Nigeria, where the Institute for Agricultural Research and Special Services has a Research Extension Liaison Section staffed with specialists, whose duties are to bring the problems of the farmers and extension workers to the research staff, and to pass on the recommendations that are the results of research to the farmers through the extension workers. The Section provides training for extension workers, and the visual aids they need in presenting modern agricultural techniques to the farmers. There is also a Rural Economy Research Unit— including an economist, sociologist, and geographer, to study local farming systems, and the factors likely to deter or influence the acceptance of new methods of farming.[1] In this way, it is hoped to ensure that research is realistic in relation to farmers' needs and constraints. The importance of an increased emphasis on rural sociology and psychology in planned innovation is now becoming more generally accepted.

The numbers of extension workers required must depend on the specific conditions—the potential for increased production,

---

[1] *Economic, cultural and technical determinants of agricultural change in tropical Africa.* Food Research Institute, Stanford University, 1969. Preliminary Report No. 6, p. 40.

degree of sophistication and technical level of farmers, complexity of new methods, mobility of extension workers, farmers' density of population. Normally in LDCs the ratio is one extension worker to between 2,000 and 5,000 farmers or sometimes even more. In Colombia, for example, during the early 1960s, there was one extension technician per 8,519 farm units, or nearly 140,000 hectares of farm land.[1] In the U.S. and Western Europe, the norm is about one extension worker for every 300 to 500 farmers, the Gezira scheme in the Sudan allowed one per 250 farmers, and not more than 100 farmers per extension worker has sometimes been suggested as a target for LDCs.

However, the provision of a complete service on this scale would be beyond the means of most LDCs. Despite political pressures, it may be necessary to concentrate services in areas of greater development potential, expanding as experience and resources allow. Paying special attention to progressive farmers can be useful, but sometimes this may have little effect, as they may merely be considered as exceptionally privileged by the rest of the local community, rather than as examples to follow. Uganda is trying seminal units in each district, from which it is hoped that innovations will spread. But in the long run strengthened extension services are likely to be essential.

The mere existence of a service, or the presence of large numbers of advisory personnel, is of course no guarantee that the service will be effective or that changes will follow. Effective extension services cannot be measured simply by numbers of agencies and technicians—the organization, administration, co-ordination activities, methods used—all are important in improving the ability of extension services to reach and help the producers.

As an example of the co-ordination problem, in Colombia, despite the limited staff, thirty-two agencies were involved in providing advisory services to farmers.[2] In Northern Ghana, although the existing level of technical knowledge offered the possibility of only very modest increases in farm output or productivity, the farmer received technical advice directly from

[1] C. Mitchell and J. Schatan: op. cit., p. 138.
[2] M. Yudelman and F. Howard: *Agricultural development and economic integration in Latin America*. Inter-American Development Bank, 1969, p. 79.

many sources. Field trials and demonstrations, essentially agronomic in nature, were handled by the Crops Research Institute and often supervised from 150 miles away, while improved seeds, which were practically non-existent, theoretically came from the Seed Multiplication Unit of the Ministry of Agriculture's Farm Supply Division. Other technical services were handled by other agencies.[1]

But rural development requires far more than the efficient co-ordination of all the official agencies operating at the village level. The process cannot be successful without the active involvement of the local population, through their village councils or any similar working organizations. Farmers' associations, commercial channels, and so on can also play important roles. In Taiwan, for example, according to Ruttan,[2] 'it seems clear that the evolution of farmers' associations into effective extension and marketing organizations together with increased incentives from the land reform of 1949–52 played significant roles in the achievement of higher rice yields'. In this case the farmer's associations employed their own extension staff, with financial help from the government.

A predominantly top-downwards development planning effort, which ignores local characteristics and the important local knowledge and enterprise of the farmers themselves, is not likely to be successful. There is still too much tendency to regard extension as telling the farmers what to do. Before farmers can be taught, there is need for a better understanding of the rationale of their farming methods, and of the problems they perceive in adopting proposed recommendations. Creating the organizational and institutional structure needed for a comprehensive rural development effort is a major challenge. Whereas in the industrial sector management and organizational skills can be imported if necessary, the framework for rural development must be a product of essentially indigenous design, if it is to deal effectively with the problems of the rural population.

[1] *Economic, cultural and technical determinants of agricultural change in tropical Africa.* Food Research Institute, Stanford University, 1969. Preliminary Report No. 7, p. 54.
[2] V. W. Ruttan: 'Engineering and agricultural development'. Conference on Engineering and the Building of Nations, Colorado, 1967, p. 32.

MECHANIZATION

Intensified agriculture requires a considerable increase in labour and land productivity. Yields must be increased through genetic improvement, cultivation techniques, weed and pest control. But this does not necessarily imply mechanization, though it may be inevitable in the long term. In some cases mechanization may be directly relevant to increased yields per acre, as in the supply of irrigation water, but often its main advantage is to allow larger areas to be covered by one farmer, possibly at greater convenience. Machines may, however, be psychologically important in getting agriculture out of the image of inferiority and drudgery which makes young people in LDCs shun it. Undoubtedly modernization of agriculture through mechanization has great appeal, but the continuing history of failures and waste of resources, quite apart from the employment aspects discussed earlier, point to the need for caution.

Common problems in mechanization schemes are an inadequate technical base for maintenance and repair, and a shortage of managerial skills. As a result a very low rate of utilization, in terms of working hours per year, is achieved, leading to high costs without commensurate returns. This can also arise from over-capitalization of small holdings. Mechanization schemes are often fostered by subsidies and duty-free imports of machinery, though an efficient strategy would possibly indicate completely reversed policies to encourage labour-intensive practices. Such mechanization schemes require large capital sums, and tie up large numbers of extension workers, but benefit only a very small number of families. It is interesting to note that in Japan it was not until 1955, when the absolute numbers engaged in agriculture began to decline appreciably, that animal draught power began to be replaced by power-driven equipment. Even now farmers in Japan rely more on power-tillers than on four-wheel tractors,[1] and these smaller machines may be more appropriate in many LDCs.

Mechanization does have advantages in operational speed, more thorough land preparation, and a capacity to deal with harder and heavier soils, but it is important to ensure that the

[1] B. F. Johnston and J. Cownie: op. cit., p. 14.

benefits do in fact outweigh the costs. Pilot trials can avoid serious waste of resources, and allow time for the development of technical and managerial skills. In most cases, though it is often regarded as a retrogressive step, animal drawn equipment is better adapted to the size of holdings, and offers many other advantages.

Labour constraints can be important in peasant agriculture, primarily as seasonal bottlenecks. Often new crops and practices have failed to achieve expected results because they involved more labour at a time when farmers already considered themselves overburdened. Low productivity in food crops may impede the development of other crops by absorbing an excessive amount of labour.

Selective mechanization can be useful in reducing these constraints but it is important to identify them correctly. An example is quoted in the Stanford study[1] at Teso in Uganda. Animal-drawn ploughs had been successfully introduced some years earlier, which had effectively eliminated the land preparation bottleneck. The provision of a tractor-hire service for land preparation in these circumstances was ineffective, as it was useless to sow more land to cotton while weeding and picking had still to be done by hand. Harvesting and subsequent operations, such as storage and first processing, are important activities where often the use of quite simple machinery can bring significant benefits. Effective mechanization requires a selective approach, and for the fullest use of available resources much greater attention needs to be paid to the overall farm management problem.

MULTIPLE CROPPING

Temperatures in the tropics allow crops to be grown all the year round, if water is available, thus making possible more than one crop in one year. Hence yields should be thought of in terms of unit of time as well as area—maximum yield per day the crop is in the field, not just per season. This is an important feature of the new varieties, which allow multiple cropping

[1] *Economic, cultural and technical determinants of agricultural change in tropical Africa.* Food Research Institute, Stanford University, 1969. Preliminary Report No. 3, p. 85.

through shorter growing periods. At IRRI, for example, a sequence involving rice and sorghum has yielded over 20 tons of food grains per hectare in one year, four times the average annual yield of corn in the U.S.A. Multiple cropping can also allow the land to be used part of the time for crops other than foods.

Many Asian countries have made considerable developments in this direction, as shown in the following table:

TABLE 3
MULTIPLE-CROPPING INDEX[a]

Country	Year	Multiple-cropping index %
Pakistan, West	1947/8	109
	1965/6	113
Pakistan, East	1947/8	130
	1965/6	137
Korea	1966	151
Taiwan	1946	118
	1966	189

[a] Total combined acreage of all crops planted in the year as percentage of total cultivated land area.

Source: *Asian Agricultural Survey*, p. 251.

Multiple cropping demands exact timing and generally a higher level of farming skills. Machines may become more important at critical periods but labour studies will be necessary to determine the best strategy. Hence, multiple cropping requires large investments in education, water resources development, fertilizers, and technological research—but can yield very high returns. According to the Asian Development Bank survey team,

so wide is the scope of multiple-cropping that it is almost always possible to find a proper combination and sequence of the right kind of crops to fit the specific needs and conditions of an area for a more efficient use of water and land resources and a higher net income to farmers. In all probability this will constitute the main direction of agricultural development in this region, after the basic needs for staple foods are largely met through intensification and when more extensive water control facilities and a larger number of photo-period insensitive short-duration crop varieties become available.[1]

[1] *Asian agricultural survey*: op. cit., p. 251.

They note, however, that very few consistent efforts have so far been made, and cropping system improvement is described as a major neglected area of research.

ECONOMIC AND INSTITUTIONAL FACTORS

The complexity of the factors which condition the acceptance of new technology has already been stressed. Economic factors influencing the adoption of new practices include infrastructure development, the demand for agricultural products, credit facilities, tenure, and government policies with regard to these specific aspects and the general role of agriculture in national development.

As peasant farmers move from subsistence production into a monetary economy, the bulk of the increase in production must be marketed, placing tremendous strains on the marketing complex to grade, process, store, transport, and finance the surplus. Transport, storage, and processing facilities are to some extent complementary, but the capacity of the overall system will need to be increased. The FAO Provisional Indicative World Plan[1] envisages that marketed output will increase three- to four-fold by 1985. The provision of services and facilities will need to keep pace with this growth, acting as both cause and effect.

It is generally agreed that post-harvest losses of agricultural products in the tropics are high. In the Philippines, post-harvest losses were estimated at 12 per cent, approximately equal to the gap between domestic rice supply and demand in 1966.[2] Bulk storage with modern equipment and procedures is efficient, and the main losses apparently occur at the village merchant level. With the larger volumes of produce coming on the market, unless storage facilities at the farm and intermediate dealers levels are improved, losses will increase. A major cause of deterioration in stored grain is insufficient drying before storage, though rats and other pests also take their toll. If grain is properly dried beforehand, cheap watertight containers can be quite effective for small-scale short-term storage. But the new seeds may worsen the situation as they sometimes need to be harvested during the monsoon season, when sun-drying is impossible. Inadequate milling facilities can also increase losses.

[1] FAO: op. cit., p. 52.   [2] Ibid., p. 31.

Though much work has been done on these problems, there is need for a considerable increase in advisory services and in research to devise cheap but effective storage and processing methods. If the steps being taken towards intensified agriculture and increased output are not to be frustrated, greater efforts must be made to reduce post-harvest losses. This is an area where the technological capabilities of industrialized countries could be extremely useful.

However, the paramount threat to the Green Revolution is increasingly the availability of markets rather than production technology. The governments of LDCs face the dilemma of maintaining a cereal price high enough to encourage efficient farmers to invest in improved technologies but not so high as to produce unmarketable surpluses.[1] The margin between scarcity and surfeit is narrow, and countries emerging from food deficit status, like those which are already self-sufficient, risk disastrously low product prices if they accelerate the application of science and technology to the agricultural sector. Food expansion beyond population growth may result in sharply declining prices. But to forego research and improvement may allow other nations the opportunity to lower costs and win export markets—technical change can significantly alter comparative advantages.

With the general adoption of modern techniques, a large expansion of food grain exports is unlikely to be profitable, and attention must be shifted from cereals to a wider range of food-stuffs—livestock, fruit and vegetables, and to other crops, product specialization and exchange. Prior to recent developments the most promising indications of yield increases through the application of modern technology to tropical agriculture related to export crops, where many significant improvements have been achieved. But for most traditional tropical export crops the rate of growth of demand in developed countries is at best relatively slow, and many face increasing competition from synthetics. To a great extent LDC earnings from agricultural exports depend on the trade and farm policies of developed countries, which can offset the comparative advantages of LDCs, as illustrated in the protection of temperate beet-sugar production against cane-sugar, which can usually be produced

[1] Lester R. Brown: op. cit., p. 97.

in tropical and sub-tropical countries at much lower costs.[1] Adverse trade terms often lead to the greater part of the benefits from technical improvements being lost to the country in which they have been applied. For example, significant increases in cocoa yields in Ghana in 1959–60, mainly through capsid control, immediately led to a drastic fall in world prices, wiping out any potential gains. Given more favourable terms, the possibilities for export crops may be exemplified by the Ivory Coast, where through the development of intensive market gardening techniques export pineapple production was increased from virtually nil in 1950 to 50 per cent of the total French market in 1966.[2] In Taiwan, from nothing in the 1950s, export earnings from canned mushrooms rose to $25 million in 1966.[3]

In emulating these examples, lack of international marketing experience is a common weakness, but there may be many other problems. An example has been cited[4] from Chile, where opportunities from the efficient production of fruits, with well-developed arrangements for handling, shipping, and marketing abroad, were stifled by export restrictions, over-valued exchange rates, and restrictions on the import of necessary inputs, tending to nullify the real international comparative advantage.

Industrial crops can provide opportunities not only for export but for local processing. Nearly 60 per cent of the total manufacturing output of Latin America is from industries using chiefly agricultural raw materials—food, beverages, tobacco, textiles, footwear and apparel, leather, rubber, paper, and wood.[5] There is considerable scope for increased regional trade, which may offer the main opportunities for expanding markets, for specialization, and more appropriate technological development. Latin America imports agricultural products to the value of $600,000,000 per annum which could be supplied from within the region without requiring the production of new commodities, and without any substantial diversion of major export

[1] FAO: *Provisional indicative world plan for agricultural development.* Vol. 2, p. 573.

[2] *Agricultural research priorities for economic development in Africa.* Abidjan, 1968, p. 459.

[3] R. L. Hough: *The J.C.R.R. experience in Taiwan and its application in other countries.* A.I.D. Discussion Paper No. 17, 1968, p. 26.

[4] *Agricultural development in Latin America in the next decade.* Inter-American Development Bank, 1967, p. 187.

[5] Ibid., p. 104.

crops from extra-regional markets.[1] West Africa imports annually some $86,000,000 worth of cereals, of which 50 per cent is rice, $44,000,000 worth of sugar and $30,000,000 of dairy products.[2]

Farmers' incomes depend on the prices of farm products and the prices of inputs. There is as yet little solid evidence on the effect of the improved cereal technologies on farm incomes. Brown[3] has attempted a comparison of net incomes with local and high-yielding varieties, allowing for additional use of water and fertilizers, and the lower prices which the new varieties can command because of consumer resistance—in the case of IR-8 rice the selling price may be as much as 30 per cent below that of traditional rice.

TABLE 4

COMPARISON OF NET INCOME PER ACRE FOR LOCAL AND HIGH-YIELDING VARIETIES [a]

	Local varieties	High-yielding varieties
Wheat		
Turkey	$32	$ 80
Pakistan	$13	$ 54
India	$17	$ 76
Rice		
West Pakistan	$25	$ 45
East Pakistan	$30	$119
Philippines	$81	$140

[a] Data are drawn from a number of sources and represent either attempts to estimate national averages or the results of surveys. The data, therefore, should be taken as indicating the orders of magnitude of net income with the prices prevailing at the time of the estimate. Within any country there is a great variation, depending upon yields and costs of inputs. Most data are for the 1968 crop year.

Source: Brown, *Seeds of change*, p. 42.

The comparison indicates a substantial increase in income, but as Brown points out:

The higher income figures do not mean that all farmers in the poor countries are going to become wealthy. They very probably do mean that social turmoil and discontent in the poor countries will be a central feature of the agricultural revolution. The attraction of

[1] M. Yudelman and F. Howard: op. cit., p. 97.
[2] *Agricultural research priorities for economic development in Africa*: op. cit., p. 79.
[3] Lester R. Brown: op. cit., p. 41.

higher income promises to become a strong force for social change in some communities where the new seeds are being planted. Traditional agriculture is being rapidly commercialised, and for all intents and purposes this is an irreversible process.

The use of modern agricultural techniques generally involves the purchase of inputs. For example, a Philippine farmer adopting IR-8 rice may find his cash costs rising from $8 to $88 per acre.[1] He may need not only short-term crop-financing, but medium- to long-term capital, as for a tubewell. Though the subject is extremely complex, there is now general recognition by national and international agencies that agricultural credit can be an important element in promoting technological change at the farm level. But the expansion of credit facilities must be linked with the provision of other services. Credit can be effective only in so far as the farmer can make proper use of it. It is not enough to make credit available, massive extension and education efforts are also needed. At the same time it must be remembered that there has been a great deal of agricultural development without credit, and the farmer's willingness to save and re-invest in his farm may be encouraged. The sequence of innovation may be important here, as indicated by the Stanford study discussed earlier (see p. 74). In institutional terms, the major difficulty in providing credit is to devise a system appropriate to the issuing and recovery of small loans involving millions of farmers. Agricultural banks have an important place, but decentralized village-level institutions may also be required, such as, for example, the rural banking system which forms part of the Comilla project in East Pakistan, where village-based co-operatives are integrated into a total co-operative system providing a range of development services, including credit.[2]

One of the strongest obstacles to the application of new technology in many countries is the system of land tenure, and improved tenure is often basic to the fuller exploitation of agricultural resources. According to the FAO, 'Land reform is likely to be required in some parts of *all* regions; but in South America a more equitable distribution of under-utilized land

[1] C. R. Wharton Jr.: *Strategies for rural development*. Agricultural Development Council, 1966, p. 18.
[2] A. H. Bunting: op. cit., p. 363.

must be considered *sine qua non* to increasing purchasing power and lifting demand constraints on a faster rate of expansion of domestic agriculture.'[1]

The question of agrarian reform is a highly intricate, essentially political problem, which goes well beyond the scope of this book. In the context of improving technology, however, two of the most important aspects may be noted, namely, security of tenure and size of holdings. Either communal or feudal forms of tenure may hinder development by not allowing a farmer a fair share of the fruits of his labour, or the security to encourage productive investment. Often the sharing arrangement between landlord and tenant is on a 50–50 crop basis, with the tenant having to meet all costs, which offers the tenant little inducement to use purchased materials such as fertilizers. The ownership of resources other than land, such as irrigation facilities, may also be important. Where widespread and largely unsecured tenancy exists, as in parts of India and Pakistan, the system may be too authoritarian to allow access to the cultivators without the landlord's permission.[2]

Fragmentation and dwarf holdings are common problems in most regions. For instance, it has been estimated that some two-thirds of the farms in Latin America are too small to offer full productive employment to the farmers and their families, and the only effective answer seems to be consolidation. While the optimum size of holding will depend on the ecological circumstances and the crops to be grown, neither vast estates, nor holdings which are too small for even one subsistence family, seem likely to offer the most efficient form of land distribution. An FAO Survey[3] has observed that most 'high value foods can be produced just as economically on family-sized farm units as they can be on larger units. In many instances, the family-sized unit, properly organised, capitalised, and educated, is more efficient than the larger farm'. But simple land redistribution within traditional institutional and administrative patterns will not be enough to transform subsistence peasants into commercial farmers. Fair prices and assured markets, credit facilities, and technical assistance are all likely to be essential.

[1] FAO: *Provisional world plan*—summary and main conclusions: op. cit., p. 61.
[2] G. Hunter: op. cit., p. 31.
[3] C. Mitchell and J. Schatan: op. cit., p. 55.

Land reform, like any other form of income redistribution, may not be compatible in the short term with maintaining a favourable investment climate for private capital. The need for agrarian reform, whether for social and political reasons or to further economic development, must be considered in each country. Undoubtedly for many areas it will be an essential operation if the rural majority are to be involved in the economic life of the country. More equitable land tenure will not only generate greater production incentives, but can lead to an increase in consumer capacity of the great mass of rural populations. Erratic or indecisive policies, however, can do more harm than good. For example, though efficient implementation of land reform with a ceiling on farm holdings should presumably encourage the Japanese/Taiwan pattern, the limited and unstable changes in India may have had the opposite effect, and may have encouraged landlords to consolidate their holdings and eject tenants.[1]

The major problems of rural development have encouraged the introduction in some countries of large-scale government plantations. But while nuclear plantations can play an important role in the introduction of new technology and the training of farmers, the expansion of both export- and import-substitution crops by smallholders has usually proved more profitable than by government plantations or farm settlements. Many African countries are now fostering the growth of industries based on locally produced agricultural raw materials from relatively small land holdings, such as palm oil in the Ivory Coast, cotton in Nigeria, and tea in Kenya. Success in this field may depend on a careful study of the economics of the industry. An important factor in the profitability of small farm tea growing was the separation by the Kenya Tea Development Authority of post-field production stages, where economies of scale are critical, from farm level operations.[2] All told, Kenya's small-scale farmers are now responsible for well over half the total value of marketed production from farms.[3]

A wide range of government policies can have a very signifi-

[1] B. F. Johnston and J. Cownie: op. cit., p. 31.
[2] *Economic, cultural and technical determinants of agricultural change in tropical Africa.* Preliminary Report No. 2, p. 77.
[3] E. R. Watts: 'Small-scale farmers help to expand production'. Special Supplement on Kenya, *The Times*, London, 20 October 1970.

cant impact on the adoption of technologies. The rapid increase in private tubewells in West Pakistan during the 1960s, for example, which were of decisive importance in the success of the new varieties, was aided by higher and more stable prices for agricultural products; lower cost power as a result of the government's electrification programme; and increased availability of pump materials due to the import liberalization programme.[1] On the other hand, excessive protection of industries may prejudice the modernization of the agricultural sector. Internal terms of trade may be unfavourable to farmers, not only because the prices of agricultural products are kept low, but because inflated prices are charged for the industrial products which the farmers need, such as fertilizers. Tax policies related to agriculture often show little concern for their effect on farmers' incentives.

Successful agricultural development can bring its own dangers. Technical advances by their nature have differential impacts, where those in an ecologically favourable situation can capitalize on new techniques. Improvements in one geographical area may worsen the economic welfare of another area. Any government which adopts a development strategy favouring the more privileged areas and farmers and indefinitely postponing the prospect of improvement for the majority of farmers and workers, not only risks its political future, but may also contribute to the political development of a revolutionary situation in the countryside.[2] An agricultural development strategy through technological improvement must therefore include plans to cope with the consequences of its success.[3]

MANPOWER

As noted by the Asian Agricultural Survey team (see p. 69), a major constraint on agricultural development is a general lack of qualified personnel. The emphasis on industrial development, and in some countries a loss of expatriates after independence, have contributed to a depressed level of agricultural science and

[1] D. G. Dalrymple: op. cit., p. 16.
[2] Francine R. Frankel: 'India's new strategy of agricultural development. Political costs of agrarian modernisation'. Journal of Asian Studies, XXVIII, No. 4, August, 1969.
[3] FAO: The State of Food and Agriculture. 1968, p. 113.

technology in many LDCs. There is an urgent need to raise the level of professional capability of agriculturalists, both for research, and for extension and advisory services. But the key problem is the low status of agriculture as a career, and a deliberate campaign may be necessary to improve the image of farming generally, and to raise the prestige of agricultural education, research, and advisory work, with due attention to the salary structure and fringe benefits. The problems of man-power and education are discussed more fully in Chapter V, but in many LDCs it seems likely that effective institutions for agricultural development will require reinforcements with both long-term staff and short-term interchanges from developed countries. While technology often cannot be transferred from temperate to tropical climates, scientific competence can.

There is room for a considerable increase in technical assistance in agriculture, but if scientists of a sufficiently high calibre are to be attracted to this work from developed countries, special arrangements may be needed to allow them to do so without disrupting their careers. Bilateral arrangements between institutions can be helpful in this respect. At present, limited career opportunities in agricultural research and extension are offered to the nationals of some developed countries, in organizations such as the French centres, e.g. ORSTOM (Office de la Recherche Scientifique et Technique Outre-Mer) and SATEC (Société d'Aide Technique et de Cooperation), and the Cotton Research Corporation based in the U.K., but a more extensive international organization might be able to attract a wider range of personnel, and might be more acceptable in LDCs.

CO-OPERATIVE RESEARCH

Limited personnel and funds have prompted suggestions that countries should pool their resources in co-operative efforts, to raise the level and quality of research, and reduce waste through duplication. Some international and regional research organizations have made impressive contributions, at relatively low cost, which stand as an example.

The impact of the international research centres supported by the Ford and Rockefeller Foundations in Mexico and the

Philippines is now well known. CIMMYT (International Maize and Wheat Improvement Centre) has developed new wheat varieties of which the world acreages in 1968/9 were ten times the area they occupy within Mexico. The Centre has built up gene pools covering such factors as disease, insect and drought resistance, protein quantity and quality, and insensitivity to day length, providing basic raw materials from which national breeders around the world can develop superior varieties for their specific conditions.

Similarly IRRI (International Rice Research Institute) was set up in 1962 to conduct basic research on all phases of rice production, management, distribution and use.

Following these successes, CIAT (International Centre for Tropical Agriculture) and IITA (International Institute of Tropical Agriculture) are now being established, in Colombia and Nigeria respectively, with similar organizations, operational strategies, and long-range commitments, but with broader multi-crop missions. Both these organizations receive support from the respective national governments, and from the Ford and Rockefeller Foundations, but have independent international status and governing boards. CIAT's programmes are directed towards a broad range of animal and crop production and utilization problems in the lowland tropics, which make up the greater part of Latin America. In Africa, there is still no satisfactory replacement for the bush fallow systems, and cropping systems involving annual food crops which are capable of maintaining high levels of sustained productivity have not yet been developed. Hence IITA is intended to increase the yields and improve the quality of food crops in the tropics, and to develop soil and crop management practices which will make possible stable, permanent, and productive agriculture.

The two new centres are intended to be complementary to each other, and to the two older centres, sharing responsibilities for research, training, and other activities pertaining to improved tropical agriculture. Their emphases will be on sharply focused production-oriented research, training for research and production specialists, assistance in co-operative research, extension and production programmes at regional, national, and local levels, and an information service.[1]

[1] *The International Institute of Tropical Agriculture.* Ford Foundation, 1969.

Another interesting new development in this area is the International Centre for Insect Physiology and Ecology (ICIPE) being established at Nairobi, Kenya, which seeks to capitalize on the wealth of research opportunities that exist in the insect and plant life of Eastern Africa. The Centre aims at creating joint projects involving scientists from both developed and developing countries on topics which are scientifically exciting and are, at the same time, urgently relevant to meeting insect control needs in Africa and the rest of the world.[1]

Apart from their contribution to training, and their seminal value as centres of excellence within LDCs, such organizations evidently have a decisive role in the solution of problems of major international importance requiring long-term inter-disciplinary research. Various other fields have been suggested for further centres, such as tropical vegetables, fruits, oil crops, arid land agriculture, and water control.

But it is important to recognize also the limitations of such specialized research centres.[2] They have demonstrated their effectiveness as a vehicle for the development and transfer of improved agricultural technology for tropical regions, and as a source of new basic concepts or principles, which will continue to have broad application. However, adaptive and protective research will still be required in every country, and will be a continual requirement to keep ahead of pests and diseases and to make further critical improvements. Local agricultural conditions demand specific attention by scientists and organizations within each country. In some countries this is a matter of special urgency following the widespread use of the new seeds. Single varieties can accelerate the biological dynamics of disease–plant relationships, and protective research is vital to forestall epidemic losses. Traditional agriculture maintains a low equilibrium level of productivity independently of research efforts, but the productivity levels of modern agriculture would decline rapidly without research backing. Thus, national research systems are essential, though these too may require international support and assistance.

A U.S. proposal of 1967 to strengthen international collabora-

---

[1] *The International Centre of Insect Physiology and Ecology. A statement of its objectives, activities and governance.* Nairobi, 1970.

[2] A. H. Moseman: op. cit., p. 92.

tion in adaptive research, with special emphasis on world centres, such as IRRI, regional centres for more specific problems in major ecological zones, and national centres for research on more specific problems, was considered by the Development Assistance Committee of OECD but the general consensus showed preference for bilateral or national arrangements. There was a general reluctance to commit long-range core support for world or regional centres, and a strong preference for maximum flexibility in bilateral collaboration.[1]

Co-operative research may be considered undesirable in some fields by LDCs themselves. Countries producing materials for highly competitive international markets might wish to limit the exchange of research findings. Reservations were expressed, for example, at the 1968 Abidjan Conference on Agricultural Research Priorities for Economic Development in Africa, though the exchange of research findings generally was considered desirable. 'It was suggested that the more fundamental or basic oriented research lent itself better to international organisations along ecological lines, but that applied (adaptive) research fell more clearly within the province of national research institutions.'[2] Many regional co-operative research arrangements, such as the West African programmes in cocoa, oil-palm and rice, have been broken-up, and there is some uncertainty about the future of East African research. There is little evidence of general co-operation, and the international centres themselves may play an important role only until national networks are more strongly developed.

FOREST AND SEA RESOURCES

Though the emphasis in this chapter has tended to be on cultivated crops, with occasional mention of livestock, agricultural development should be construed in the widest sense. For many LDCs, biological natural resources—including farms, forests, rivers, and seas, wild life, and tourist amenities—offer the main source of increased wealth, at least in the short term. Forest and fish resources have often been neglected, and merit much closer attention. In these, as in other areas, technological

[1] Ibid., p. 94.
[2] *Agricultural research priorities for economic development in Africa*: op. cit., p. 22.

change demands a systems approach covering social, economic and political factors as well as improved technology.

The demand for forest products is increasing steadily, particularly as industrial raw materials. In the preface to a study, *World Trends and Prospects: Wood*,[1] the Director-General of FAO said: 'The evidence assembled in the study points up the rapid rate at which the industrial wood sector is growing. In the decade to 1961, the quantity of wood used annually for industrial purposes grew by about 25%: in the subsequent 14 years, it will probably grow by nearly 45%.' Demand is shifting from unprocessed to processed wood products, and, among the latter, from solid to reconstituted wood products such as particle board and paper.

Trade in forest products will play an expanding role in satisfying the world's future wood needs, offering unusually favourable opportunities for expansion in LDCs' exports. There is a very rapidly growing trade in wood from those countries endowed with large resources of tropical hardwood timbers, while other LDCs are proving to be singularly well-favoured to establish low-cost fast-growing man-made forests which promise to become an increasingly important element of wood supply in the future. At the same time wood-using industries are among the first which can be established to substitute for imported goods as the economy develops.

If the land allocated to forestry is already forested, management for increased and sustained productivity should be based on a scientific understanding of the composition, structure, and dynamics of the forests; a wide range of scientific skills is required. The problems involved in establishing a new forest in a cleared area or, as is often required, in an arid zone or on a degraded treeless area, more closely resemble those of agriculture. Knowledge of soils and physiological relations of the young trees to the soil and to the micro-climate are needed. It may be necessary to use fertilizers, irrigation, cover-crops and pesticides. As the costs of establishing and tending a new forest are considerable and the financial returns delayed for many years, it is of the greatest importance that the planted trees should be of the best possible genetic constitution, with the fastest possible growth rate compatible with quality. Thus

[1] FAO: *World trends and prospects: Wood*. 1967.

tree-breeding must be undertaken on a national or regional basis.

The full exploitation of sea resources similarly requires a considerable body of scientific knowledge based on local conditions. But the limiting factors are likely to be the heavy investments required in infrastructure and equipment, as fisheries move from coastal to offshore and deep-sea areas. Modern ocean fisheries require an urban rather than a rural base of operations, involving motorized vessels, fishing harbours, shore facilities, cold storage, and access to markets. Steps must be taken to ensure that the catch is fully utilized, whether by domestic consumption or by processing and export.

Certain forms of environment spoilation may be more acute in LDCs than they are in developed countries. A good example is soil erosion, which under conditions of high or irregular rainfall can be very acute. Effective and scientifically based land management—including agricultural land, forests and inland waters, is needed to deal with this problem. The very fact that LDCs often still have large areas of natural vegetation and its associated animal life involves these countries in problems of conservation which must be regarded as a part of rational usage. The natural environment is fragile and it must be scientifically understood if it is to be managed, developed, or even conserved properly. The importance of biological natural resources, and their effective management and use, suggests that a significant proportion of the scientific activity of an LDC should, for economic reasons, be devoted to environmental studies.

IV   Industrialization and Research

INTRODUCTION

Accelerated industrialization is considered by most LDCs as the main key to economic development and social progress. It offers not only economic growth and a general improvement in living standards, but also an effective means of transforming and modernizing traditional economies and societies. Substantial efforts have therefore been devoted to industrial development. Investment in the manufacturing sector of LDCs as a whole runs at about $9 billion per annum, and industry is growing at an annual rate of 7 per cent.[1] This is a tremendous achievement, and compares very favourably with the industrial growth rate in developed countries of almost 6 per cent per annum. However, in absolute terms, given the narrow base, progress is slow, and LDCs still account for only 5 per cent of the world's output of manufactured goods.

Understandably, in few countries has industrialization been an integrated organic process. The problems of high population growth, lack of skills at all levels, deficient infrastructure and limited capital, particularly foreign exchange, have been compounded by adverse trade trends, comparatively small domestic markets for manufactured products, and an inability to compete with advanced countries on world markets. The process has often been inadequately planned, with little selectivity or recognition of industrial systems or markets, and the results have been poor. Progress has sometimes been hampered by a lack of continuity in political decision making. In most LDCs the benefits of a growing industrial sector have reached only a small section of the population, as, relative to the capital investment involved, modern industry can offer only limited direct employment opportunities. The resources already invested in industry are often inefficiently used, and there is a prime need to improve performance through better management, better

[1] UNIDO: 'Report of the International Symposium on Industrial Development', held in Athens, 1967. Reference ID/B/21 of 2 February 1968, Annex 2, p. 11.

utilization of existing capacity, and a more adequate infrastructure, particularly the servicing institutions required by industry.

With the concentration of effort on industrial development in some countries, the agricultural sector has been relatively neglected as it seemed to offer little prospect of being a mainspring of economic growth, or even of producing sufficient food. However, technological developments in agriculture now encourage a more hopeful attitude to the food problem, and the sector is itself creating a need for industrialization to supply inputs such as fertilizers and pesticides and to process agricultural products, while offering expanding domestic markets through increased employment and purchasing power.

Development of industry, of agriculture, and of other productive sectors are now seen to be interdependent and complementary. While substantial industrial–urban development may be inevitable and necessary for economic growth in the long term, in the short term the appropriate emphasis to be accorded to industry or agriculture will depend on the particular circumstances in each country, its stage of development, and the alternatives available, especially the exploitation of mineral resources. In most LDCs, agriculture and agro-based industries will necessarily play a leading role for many years. Where agriculture accounts for a significant share of the national product, and the rural areas may have as much as 80 per cent of the population, however fast industry is growing it cannot alone achieve a satisfactory level of economic growth. Agricultural and rural development is essential to broaden domestic markets and to allow the expansion of local industry through the increased buying power of the bulk of the people. At the same time, a vital agriculture can help to keep the urban drift within manageable proportions and can generate increased domestic savings for further investment. Any policy for industrialization needs, therefore, to be closely associated with parallel, and in many cases much greater efforts to modernize agriculture and develop the rural areas.

To meet an increasing domestic demand for manufactured products, without worsening balance of payments problems, countries must either increase exports of products for which the demand is rising, or themselves produce manufactured goods to satisfy home markets. Generally in LDCs the main source of foreign exchange to pay for imported manufactured products has been the export of primary products. But as a result of the development of synthetic substitutes, trade policies, and economies in the use of materials in developed countries, the trends of world demand for tropical agricultural products have been mostly adverse and among primary products trends consistently favourable to LDCs have been largely restricted to the increasing consumptions of minerals, fuels, and timber. Import substitution has therefore been the normal first step towards industrialization, generally concentrating initially on light consumer goods for direct consumption—textiles, foods, and packing or assembly operations on imported bulk materials or components.

Many light industries have limited technical content, and involve relatively restricted technological inter-relationships, though some, such as electronics or cameras, may depend on very advanced technology. Apart from essential basic heavy industries such as power generation, it seems, therefore, realistic in the early stages to concentrate on light and traditional industries, but giving due attention to quality standards, costs, and improved production methods, and at the same time building up training facilities, technological abilities, working efficiency, supporting financial arrangements, and so on. As skills are developed locally techniques can become more complex, and the production scale tends to become larger. According to an EEC report,

econometric studies show that on average, at a stage of development corresponding to a per capita income of $100, 68% of industrial output will be consumer goods and only 12% capital goods. On the other hand, when development has reached a stage where per capita income is $600, the share of capital goods in industrial production will have risen to 35%, while consumer goods will account for only 43%. The share of intermediate goods varies within fairly narrow limits.[1]

At each stage of development a country will need to strike its own appropriate balance between consumer, intermediate, and capital goods.

[1] EEC: *Industrialisation schemes for the African States associated with the Community.* Commission of the European Communities, June 1967, p. 12.

Import substitution can create a useful infrastructure of production facilities and entrepreneurs, working capacity and experience. But it eventually runs into problems through the limited size of domestic markets. With light consumer goods, low costs can often be achieved even at low volumes of production. But with more sophisticated products, using modern techniques, and in most heavy industries, economies of scale become more important, and efficient production requires larger markets. Except perhaps for the largest LDCs this implies either regional co-ordination and specialization, or entry into the international trade in manufactures. But until a sufficient level of technical competence is attained, the prospects in highly competitive world markets may be limited, and increased regional trade may offer the best avenue to industrial development. Arthur Lewis has observed that 'if developing countries want to grow faster than the developed world, they will have to trade relatively less with the developed world and relatively more with each other'.[1]

The choice of an appropriate technology to suit local needs is discussed in a later section. There is some scope for adapting modern technologies to suit the needs of small markets, but often this can be done only at considerably increased production costs. Allowing competitive market conditions may then run counter to the requirements for economies of scale. In Iran, for example, it has been reported[2] that there are thirteen car assembly plants, serving a relatively small market, with the result that the final products cost twice as much as on the open world market.

Import substitution can lead to a distorted production structure. Protection may be essential if new industries are to develop, but it can be misused—in Brazil for example the highest protection tends to be given to long established industries which should by now have become competitive. Import substitution and excessive protection may tend to promote a passive attitude to the application of technology to industrial development. In many LDCs the market is characterized by a strong demand in

---

[1] W. A. Lewis: *The development process*. Executive Briefing Paper, No. 2, United Nations Centre for Economic and Social Information, 1970.

[2] *Industrialisation in Developing Nations*. Engineering Foundation Research Conference, University School, Milwaukee, August 1969, Summary Report, p. 13.

relation to a limited supply in a highly protected environment. Under these circumstances there is little inclination to innovate, and businessmen prefer to rely on buying from advanced countries proven techniques, not necessarily the most appropriate, the costs of which can be passed directly to the customers, and which offer virtually certain financial returns in the short term. Over-dependence on imported technology, unsupported by local adaptive R and D, may limit the exploitation of certain natural resources, because the technology was developed in another country where these resources were not available, and may, through restrictive controls imposed by the suppliers, act as a brake to the growth of manufacturing for export. But technological dependence is not in itself a hindrance to development, and, as discussed below, the proper use of imported technology is an important feature of development strategy. The hindrance is the lack of technological development and adaptation, to gear the technology to the combination of natural resources and factors of production locally available. A primary aim in industry is technical competence, at every stage from the purchase of raw materials, the selection of processes and equipment, through to marketing and sales. A high level of competence may be impossible without at least some adaptive research.

This becomes increasingly important as production moves from import substitution to exports which must be competitive in regional or world markets. Even here, technological knowledge is not necessarily a major limiting factor hindering development. According to an UNCTAD study in Brazil,[1] the factors limiting exports were exchange costs, the marketing system abroad and quality control, rather than raw materials, production capacity, or technical knowledge. For most potential increases in exports, technical knowledge was rated adequate or abundant.

Within an industrializing country, technology levels may vary widely, even within a single industry. In some Latin American countries, the value added per worker in textile mills covers a

[1] UNCTAD: 'Short- and medium-term prospects for exports of manufactures from selected developing countries—Brazil'. Background paper prepared for the Athens Symposium by UNCTAD Secretariat. UNIDO Reference ID/CONF.1/ B.30 of 26 July 1967.

range of one to five. This is not necessarily undesirable. Technological pluralism can be used deliberately, as earlier in Japan,
to help maintain employment, but efficiency is important
whether techniques are labour-intensive or capital-intensive.
An ECLA survey[1] of industrial development in Latin America
has pointed out that technology levels are associated with
market competition, the age of the industry, sources of finance,
connections with foreign firms, the nature of the enterprise, and
the business flair of the management. Little attention is paid
usually to choosing techniques more compatible with the
characteristics and resources of the region. In the absence of
national programmes or policies for the application of technology to development, the selection of manufacturing processes
and plant sizes depends entirely on the individual manufacturers. Technologies chosen are often inappropriate, so that
excessive capital is employed, while capacities are grossly under-
used. The process may be aggravated by institutional defects—
the nature of enterprises, managerial capacity, market
shortcomings, which often have a more serious impact than
technological dependence.

The report concludes that one of the major objectives in
Latin American industry must be to increase efficiency and
productivity. While this would appear obvious, its importance
is not always recognized. Labour productivity is generally low
and capital inefficiently used. In many cases, improvements in
entrepreneurial level and organizational methods are the prime
factors. Under-used capacity in capital goods manufacture may
be due to lack of market knowledge, lack of finance to allow
credit terms, or the fact that the smallest available plant is over-
large. The combination of antiquated technologies, low labour
productivity, and poor capital utilization inevitably leads to
increased production costs and selling prices, which may be
two or three times above U.S. prices. Similarly, a study of the
process plant industry in India[2] has emphasized that ineffi-
ciencies of planning, procurement, execution, and operation
can have a disastrous effect on plant profitability. 'Delays and

---

[1] ECLA: *The United Nations Second Development Decade. Industrial Development in
Latin America.* Economic Commission for Latin America. E/CN.12/830 of 13 March
1969.

[2] *The process plant industry in India.* An Indo-British Survey, March 1970.

under-utilisation can between them destroy the potential advantage of large-scale investment and modern technology.'

Management is one of the most decisive elements of modern industry, as without proper management resources are unlikely to be used in the most effective way. Efforts to improve management capacity and introduce modern management techniques are a vital part of any industrialization programme. It has been suggested[1] that the prevalence of basic work simplification and efficiency concepts and attitudes may be more important to the competitive posture of the U.S.A. than the most glamorous modern technologies. But as with other forms of operational technology, the effective transfer of managerial skills and attitudes is likely to require adaptation to suit local circumstances. Some aspects of this problem are examined in Chapter V.

TECHNOLOGICAL INNOVATION

Stress was laid in Chapter I on the key role of technological innovation. Economic growth through technological development depends on continual innovation in the form of new or improved products and processes, and the general acceptance of these innovations throughout the production structure. Charpie[2] has classified technological innovations as (1) those which bring about productivity gains, (2) those which represent new contributions to existing products, processes or industries, and (3) those which express themselves in the spectacular creation of completely new industries. As this writer has suggested, the scope for the third class of innovation is likely to be small in the less industrialized economies, but the productivity gain type of economic growth, which usually entails a lower cost and produces a higher benefit-to-cost ratio, will probably be the dominant vehicle of economic growth.

Innovations may be derived from technological advances resulting from local research efforts or from advances made

[1] J. R. Quinn: Discussion at a Symposium on 'Technology and World Trade', U.S. Dept. of Commerce/National Bureau of Standards, November 1966. NBS Misc. Pub. 284, p. 100. Prepared for UNESCO Symposium on *The role of science and technology in economic development*, September 1968.

[2] R. A. Charpie: 'Technological innovation and the international economy'. In *Technological Innovation and the Economy*, edited by Maurice Goldsmith, Wiley—Interscience, 1970.

elsewhere. No country can afford to be self-sufficient in this respect and each country must aim for the optimum combination, in the particular circumstances, of its own R and D and the assimilation of scientific and technological advances made in other countries. Every country, however developed, attempts to take advantage of both internal and external sources to gain the fullest possible benefits from modern science and technology. For most LDCs, there are not enough qualified people to allow a comprehensive R and D system, and the prime need is to ensure the full and effective use, through adaptation, of foreign technology and science.

But strategy with regard to imported and home-grown scientific and technological advances is only part of the picture. The economy benefits only when these advances have been incorporated into production and they are valueless unless followed by the innovative and diffusion stages. The process has been seen as analagous to biological evolution.

The phase of *mutation* corresponds to the first half of the research and development operation, during which new techniques and processes are devised and prepared for testing and costing; the phase of *selection* is the one at which, within some specific area of application, the techniques or processes in question are shown to be feasible, both in technical and in economic terms; while the final phase of *diffusion* and *dominance* is that in which these skills spread into the general body of industrial and engineering techniques.[1]

By itself the 'mutation' stage is unproductive. For economic development it is essential to consider the obstacles to innovation and diffusion, and mechanisms which will facilitate them. Without this, neither indigenous R and D nor imported technologies can have a sustained effect.

In market economies, innovations stem from a continuous demand pressure on entrepreneurs for new products and processes. Successful innovating businesses develop and maintain close communications between marketing and technical personnel, so as to bring together a real or anticipated demand and a feasible technical solution. Even where there is no commercial market to which to respond, as in defence research, an

[1] S. Toulmin: 'Innovation and the problem of utilisation'. In *Factors in the Transfer of Technology*, edited by W. H. Gruber and D. G. Marquis, MIT Press, 1969, p. 25.

attempt is made to match recognized needs with technical capabilities, through the application of systems analysis, relating specifications of future weapons, technical resources, and financial considerations. In developed planned economies, planning procedures provide similar pressures for innovation.

But in the typical mixed economy of an LDC these pressures are much weaker. In these circumstances, it is difficult to ensure that local R and D is relevant to national needs, and one of the basic problems of LDCs is to find means of effectively linking R and D to the production system. This presents a serious problem even in an industrialized country like the U.K., when it comes to harnessing government-financed research to industry. Where possible, an environment needs to be formed which will encourage innovation, so as to generate a demand for new technology, and create conditions where technology will be pulled into industry, not pushed from the outside. Entrepreneurs, able to see the potential value of some resource and follow the idea through to commercialization, have a vital role in this process. The increasing trend towards export-oriented industries which will have to face international competition will promote innovation. But market mechanisms may not be sufficient to take full advantage of relatively unexplored natural resources, and science policy planning in relation to economic development must help close this gap. Under the circumstances, in most LDCs, innovative efforts will need some measure of central planning.

The U.S. National Academy of Sciences has taken part in several workshops in various LDCs to consider means of making R and D more productive in industry. The workshops have revealed[1] that few nations have a development plan with a related scientific and technological plan, specified priorities and a system for evaluating accomplishments. Frequent problem areas are the absence of a satisfactory organization for formulating national science and technology policies, and the lack of communications between government, universities and industry. Without this interaction, industrial management lacks interest in local R and D, which itself lacks market knowledge and industrial know-how. For successful innovation R and D must be fully integrated into the production and marketing system.

[1] *Industrialisation in Developing Nations*: op. cit., p. 5.

At the technical level, a country's capacity to exploit modern technology depends on the number and distribution of scientists, technologists, technicians, and engineers. Trained people are needed throughout industry to make use of and improve on technological advances. Fully effective use of imported technology demands an ability to know what is required and how to put it to use. Where an enterprise has a sufficient cadre of technicians the imported know-how will not only be quickly put to full use, but it will generate new ideas and further improvements. An ability to use a relatively low-level degree of technological knowledge in routine production, distribution, and service industries, which normally make up the greater part of the manufacturing contribution to the GNP, may be far more important than the most advanced technology.

Industry will require the support of institutions, with qualified staff, to help in the selection of the most appropriate technology, its adaptation to suit local needs and conditions, and the diffusion of the resulting technologies. The less advanced a country is, the more the emphasis in its scientific and technological activities needs to be on the diffusion of information, and on technical advisory and other extension services, with R and D primarily concerned with supporting and exploiting the transfer of technology.

TRANSFER MECHANISMS

All countries have a strong interest in arrangements for the international diffusion of technical knowledge. Scientific information is transferred by published papers, private communications between scientists, and by conferences. Scientists in LDCs have the disadvantages of physical isolation, and often lack foreign exchange funds for travel to conferences or to buy scientific journals, but there is no inherent problem of access. Technology is transferred in different ways. Published information is not so helpful, and other mechanisms are more important—movements of people, technical co-operation programmes, licences, patent agreements, and foreign investment. One of the major avenues for technology transfer is through the purchase of capital equipment and machinery.

But while basic requirements for technology can generally be met through access to published material, foreign training, the activities of technological research and information centres, the employment of foreign technicians, and the straight purchase of foreign know-how as in the form of patents and licences, operative technology for enterprises of more than a rudimentary character cannot generally be acquired in this manner.[1] The efficient application of more sophisticated technology also involves the disciplines of management, the organization of production, and marketing of finished products. Such technology is very much the creation of the business enterprise, whether public or private, within which the interaction and teamwork of management, research, production, and sales stimulate the development and implementation of a constant stream of innovation. Hence, as a primary source of managerial and technical know-how, modern industrial enterprises in LDCs will often seek an arrangement with an enterprise engaged in a similar line of activity in a developed country. The international corporation with its advantages of capital, skills, and markets has an important role in this process.

Even within the context of a highly developed industrial economy, technology transfer from the laboratory into the production mechanism is not necessarily spontaneous. When transistors were first developed in the U.S.A., the potential value of the research results achieved at the Bell Laboratories was not immediately recognized by other industrial engineers and research scientists. It required a major educational effort by Bell to introduce to the science and business communities a sense of the potentialities implicit in the new transistor technology, and the active use of their scientific and engineering skills to teach and train those who wished to learn the science and know-how of the transistor.[2] Similarly, when radio-active isotopes first became available in quantity and at low prices, 'scientists did not grasp the research potential and industrialists did not grasp the technological possibilities'. A special agency had to be established to disseminate knowledge concerning and

---

[1] 'Basic problems in the transfer of technology to developing countries'. Report by the Fiscal and Financial Branch of the UN Dept. of Economic and Social Affairs, for UNCTAD, Second Session. TD/37, 22 December 1967.

[2] R. A. Solo: *Technology transfer—a universal process*. Symposium on 'Inducing technological change in developing nations', Robert Solo and Everett Rogers (eds.), Michigan State University Press (forthcoming).

to promote the use of radio-isotope technology. These two examples represent successful transfers of major science-based technologies, but the important point is that in neither case did dissemination occur spontaneously. A positive and planned effort directed to this specific end was required.

Similarly, a NASA study on the possible use of U.S. space technology in Brazil[1] concluded that successful applications depended not only on the identification and availability of suitable technology but also on the existence of viable transfer mechanisms. Effective technology transfer programmes require significant commitments in both the disseminating and the recipient nations.

The difficulties of transfer, even with goodwill on both sides, may be illustrated by the transfer of a manufacturing capability for a particular type of aeroplane, by mutual government agreement, from an American to a Japanese firm under a co-production arrangement. A study of this case[2] concluded that technology was easily transferred for the airframes of the plane, transferred with difficulty for the engines, while very little of the technology for the electronics was transferred at all during the period of the arrangement. The ease of transferring manufacturing technology appeared to depend significantly upon the amount of general knowledge that had to be included in the transfer. Japan of course has a sophisticated industrial economy and in general ample engineering and technical skills to absorb foreign techniques, but in this case, through lack of previous experience with the particular type of electronic equipment involved, transfer of this manufacturing technology was less successful than for airframes or engines. In general it would seem that the wider the disparities in economic or technical levels between associating or co-operating partners, the less successful the relationship is likely to be.

At the second session of UNCTAD in New Delhi, 1968, the question of the transfer of technology to LDCs was raised, as

[1] Pilot Study—*Space technology transfer and developing nations*. Prepared by A. D. Little Inc. for the National Aeronautics and Space Administration, Washington, August 1968.

[2] G. R. Hall and R. E. Johnson: 'Transfer of U.S. aerospace technology to Japan'. Conference on 'The technology factor in international trade', October 1968. Vol. 22 of the Universities–National Bureau Conference Series, Raymond Vernon (ed.), Columbia University Press, 1970.

indeed it had been at the first session, and it was considered that existing arrangements were not adapted to LDC needs. The Trade and Development Board are now examining avenues for improvement. Various proposals have been made, including the establishment of technology transfer centres, as suggested by the U.N. Advisory Committee on Science and Technology,[1] to act as intermediaries tying together national centres and relevant foreign sources of technological information and operating know-how, and ensuring adaptation to local needs and effective application by domestic users. No comprehensive feasibility studies of this proposal have, however, yet been attempted.

The Industrial Information Service of UNIDO attempts to tap the technical and industrial knowledge of developed countries. The service was started in 1966, and now deals with over sixty inquiries a month from LDCs, but it operates with very limited resources. Such an information network might serve a useful purpose, though a more detailed appraisal of needs and mechanisms seems necessary. The evidence suggests that the transfer of technology requires far more than routing information through a communications system. Any enlargement of international agencies needs to be paralleled by stronger national institutions, which can make fuller use of existing information sources. As a recent paper has commented in relation to the less developed OECD countries, 'one might perhaps speculate on the extent to which foreign investment and licensing would be reduced if industry in the five countries sought out and made effective use of all the technological information which is *freely* available'.[2]

The U.N. Advisory Committee on Science and Technology took the view that

the problem of transfer as such was a minor one, and that the real task was to build up science and technology infrastructure without which inefficient use and costly waste would be involved in importing technology. The real bottleneck for the developing countries

[1] UN Advisory Committee on the Application of Science and Technology to Development, Third Report, May 1966.

[2] E. P. Hawthorne: 'The transfer of Technology'. Report prepared for a Seminar on the Transfer of Technology to Less Industrialised Countries, held at Istanbul, October 1970, under the auspices of the OECD's Technical Co-operation Programme.

was not the lack of availability in technology or its cost. It was rather the lack of domestic ability to absorb technology in an efficient manner.[1]

INTERNATIONAL CORPORATIONS

Capital transfers have an important role to play in development, particularly as a conveyor of technology. The special usefulness of international corporations depends on a combination of capital, advanced technology, and access to world markets—all vitally important to LDCs.

Any government would understandably prefer to acquire the capital, technology, and markets it needs without conceding ownership to foreigners, but the actual outcome usually depends on the results of a bargaining process. Large domestic markets will strengthen a country's bargaining position, while an adverse balance of payments position or a need for very advanced technologies will be weakening factors. The position is, however, not static and changes with time—for example, if a country's industrialization policy becomes less concerned with import substitution and is directed more towards export into competitive markets, the need for more advanced technology may lessen the capacity to drive a hard bargain.

LDCs thus face a dilemma between the benefits which an international organization can offer and some possible loss of control over part of the national economy. National sovereignty may be affected, as for example when General Motors decided not to export from its Australian subsidiary to Japan, but to leave the Japanese market to its Californian plants, Australia was left very exposed for it had no other Australian produced car to send to the Japanese market at a time when Japanese cars were flooding Australia.[2] Reinvestment of profits, coupled with the modern trend for corporations to become involved in the general progress of the host country, may lead to a progressive increase in foreign dominance and control of the economy, with an ultimate danger of a reverse flow of funds greater than the original investment. It has been claimed in the case of Peru[3] that, over the past twenty years, for every $30 in foreign

[1] UN Advisory Committee on the Application of Science and Technology to Development. Eleventh session, April 1969.

[2] Peter Parker: *The Times*, London, 10 November 1969.

[3] Reported in *The Times*, London, 10 August 1970.

investment, $100 has left the country in royalties, profits, and debt servicing.

Most countries, highly developed as well as less developed, show some resistance to foreign corporations, and their fears are often justifiable. International corporations have an important role to play, and sometimes a socially acceptable rate of economic growth may be unattainable without their contribution of funds and technologies. But this contribution will be acceptable only if the corporations recognize the legitimate interests and aspirations of host countries, and take a long-term view of their own interests. It is probably inevitable that corporations are judged not in economic cost-benefit terms, but in political or emotional terms.

Foreign investment capital may bring not only a transfer of technological know-how and access to new research developments, but also a transfer of business technology—skills of production, accounting, marketing, finance, organization, and management, developed in a competitive environment. A priority task in LDCs is the fostering of managerial skills, and international corporations can make a significant contribution in this area. For example, as a result of extensive management training programmes, Imperial Chemical Industries (India) Ltd. had in 1969 only 11 non-Indians in a total management staff of 663, with plans to reduce to two by 1974. The benefits may not be limited to the subsidiaries alone. Corporations may need to devote considerable technical and managerial skills to help develop local supplier firms, as with quality control, material standards and laboratory testing.

In their relations with international corporations, LDCs may gain advantages through thinking less exclusively in fiscal terms, and paying more attention to the contribution which corporations can make in terms of personnel training, management, participation in research and educational activities, the development of suppliers, and customer service activities. This implies a positive approach to the transfer of technology generally, with more active policies for the acquisition and diffusion of technology.

Some countries complain of the reluctance of international corporations to undertake local research. From the corporation's point of view this may be a question of scale of operations relative to the minimum critical size of effective research effort, though most will find some measure of local adaptive development work advisable. Some countries also insist on the transfer of a design capability, as in the arrangements between Yugoslavia and the Fiat Motor Company of Italy. But while local R and D within an industrial corporation may have long-term advantages to the host country, particularly in training, it is well to recognize that in the short term it may absorb scientists and technologists who could be more usefully employed elsewhere, and the results will become available to all the corporation's subsidiaries, not only locally.

To reduce the tensions and conflicts, various proposals have been made for some kind of partnership between foreign and local interests, such as management contracts, co-production schemes, and joint ventures. Joint capital participation may not necessarily be more favourable towards LDCs. Parent companies tend to take a more lenient attitude towards wholly-owned subsidiaries than to joint ventures with regard to royalties and access to research results. Wholly-owned subsidiaries are often given a larger export role than joint ventures. Many international corporations consider a significant financial involvement essential for the close and sustained relationship necessary for the effective transfer of technology and associated manufacturing and marketing capabilities. Too much insistence on joint ownership may lead to firms being unwilling to invest.

But in recent years the skills to build, equip, staff, and manage modern industrial plants are becoming increasingly available without yielding ownership to a foreign manufacturing firm, through the international sale of industrial services. Co-operation between State enterprises in Eastern Europe and private enterprises in Western countries, such as the Fiat-Yugoslavia arrangement mentioned above, offer a demonstration of such international associations.

PATENTS, LICENCES, AND KNOW-HOW AGREEMENTS

One of the most common forms of technology transfer is through the purchase of patents or licences. It has already been argued that the proper exploitation of the developed countries'

9

technology represents a sound strategy for LDCs. They cannot afford to re-invent everything for themselves, nor do they need to pass through all the technological stages which have preceded modern processes. Until resources permit an adequate indigenous scientific and technological infrastructure, an LDC might reasonably spend on patents and licences at least as much, if not a great deal more, than in the performance of its own R and D.

But there is justifiable concern, not only with regard to the direct costs in respect of royalties, patents, and trade marks paid to foreign enterprises, and associated technical assistance costs, but also with the restrictions often included in contracts concerning the size of the market, and with the possible social costs from the use of unsuitable techniques.

A preliminary study in Mexico,[1] carried out under the auspices of the U.N. Economic and Social Council, showed that contractual arrangements between enterprises for technology transfer are extremely complex and in most cases derive from a long bargaining process. Even relatively simple arrangements involve a host of elements such as definitions of products, sales territories, fees and down payments, equity interest, stock acquisition rights, and tax liabilities. The absolute level of down payments and fees or their expression in terms of percentage of sales, gross profits or net profits, offers very little indication about the actual burden of the contract. Undue financial sacrifices may appear not only in the form of excessive royalties, but also in excessive prices paid for materials or components or for the services of technicians obtained from the patentee.

Larger firms, whether public or private, show an ability to shop around for technology and diversify their sources, often using international consultants, so as to prevent many abuses. The main problems arise with small or medium firms, which often prefer a package deal with a single external agency, despite the potential danger of corporate links and control, and, through lack of technical knowledge, may end up at the mercy of foreign designers and contractors. This is an area

[1] 'Arrangements for the transfer of operative technology to developing countries'. UN Economic and Social Council, E/4452, 26 March 1968. Add. 3, Annex 3. 'Case study of Mexico'.

where national advisory services can be useful, backed by the research organizations discussed below, and by local consulting firms.

The governments of the LDCs have a legitimate interest in preventing excessive exploitation of their one-sided techno-logical and financial dependence. Of particular concern to them are undue financial sacrifices resulting in balance of payments burdens, and unduly restrictive features, especially relating to exports, which diminish the benefits of introducing the patented innovation. One possible approach is the central screening and control of licence agreements, as for example applied in Japan's Ministry of International Trade and Industry. But the financial terms of these agreements may be highly complex, and their effective control calls for considerable administrative resources and flexibility.

In a study by the U.N. Secretary-General on the role of patents in the transfer of technology[1] it was concluded that the effect of higher prices specifically due to patent protection is almost impossible to disentangle from higher prices due to such factors as exclusive know-how, trade secrets, restrictive practices, or the dominant market position of the supplier, all of which are intrinsically unrelated to the patent system. Hence measures directly affecting price levels or general antitrust legislation may be an economically more effective and administratively more feasible technique of coping with the problems than legislation devoted specifically to the patent system.

The governments of more developed countries can assist by inducing patentees not to be unduly restrictive in the conditions and terms on which they are willing to sell technology to LDCs: a variety of policy measures ranging from domestic compensa-tion of patentees, provision of international funds for this purpose, equivalent investment guarantees and legislation against restrictive practices applying to business operations abroad have been proposed for this purpose.

However, licence agreements, know-how contracts, and patents together constitute only a part of the total techno-logical knowledge which should and to a large extent does flow to LDCs. The role of patents is limited partly because much

---

[1] *The role of patents in the transfer of technology to developing countries*. Report of the Secretary-General, United Nations, 1964.

of the technology required by these countries is not at the latest stage of technological advance which is covered by patents, and partly because some LDCs lack so much in general know-how and management experience, that the knowledge covered by patents alone is usually not sufficient for the introduction of new products and processes. The study of the U.N. Secretary-General cited above considered that the question was best examined in the broader context of facilitating the transfer of technology in general, and enhancing the ability of the LDCs to adapt and use such foreign technology in the implementation of their development programmes.

The patent system was designed in developed countries to encourage R and D and increase the flow of inventions. This represents something of a paradox in that the system designed to this end 'allows the patent holder to restrict the diffusion of new inventions until the inventor has reaped his reward by exploiting his short-term monopolistic position'.[1] In so far as the system offers protection, it slows down the diffusion of patented inventions, but lack of this protection, or some other form of compensation, may hinder technological development. In LDCs patents issued to national and resident inventors can help to promote the development of an indigenous technology. The importance of this may be limited in the early stages of development, but the patent system seems a necessary protection to encourage the flow of technology generally from developed countries, and at a later stage may help to produce counter-balancing returns through cross-licensing.

Most LDCs are short of both the specialized personnel and the funds needed to strengthen their patent facilities. The United International Bureaux for the Protection of Intellectual Property (BIRPI) has given active assistance to LDCs in the field of patent legislation and industrial property matters. The current BIRPI plan for a Patent Co-operation Treaty has among its aims the possibility of making available to LDCs, for the purpose of the examination of foreign and national applications for patents, the resources of the major examining offices in the developed countries.

---

[1] M. Kranzburg and C. W. Pursell: *Technology in Western Civilization*, Vol. 1, O.U.P., 1967, p. 518.

CONSULTANTS

Industrial and management consultants can provide another most effective form of technology transfer. They may offer various levels of service, ranging from direct assistance to a government in establishing an integrated industrial development plan, to specific technical studies for a single industrial enterprise. Expertise may include design and engineering, technological, economic, management and training services.

A UNIDO manual on the use of consultants in developing countries[1] lists the following possible advantages from the use of consultants.

1. Shortening the time needed for the implementation of projects.
2. Obtaining specialized skills and know-how.
3. Finding a fresh approach to established practices.
4. Obtaining independent evaluations and recommendations.

But it has been pointed out[2] that the consultant, as an instrument of development, has the weakness of all *ad hoc* transitory agencies. Because they are without continuing long-range responsibility, their work may be quick and shallow. Most significantly, 'They build for the developing society, but they do not build into the developing society the essential competence to develop and grow continuously. They may offer a too-easy alternative for the essential task of creating an indigenous capacity for choice and action.'

As with most other transfer mechanisms, no satisfactory cost-benefit appraisals of the value of consultants appear to have been made. But there are many examples of long-term associations between consultants and their clients in LDCs, such as the sister relationship between the Battelle Memorial Institute and the Korean Institute of Science and Technology, and Arthur D. Little's involvement in Algeria's development programme. Provision of such services at the individual firm level, particularly for the smaller firm, needs great care to ensure that the

[1] *Manual on the use of consultants in developing countries*, UNIDO, 1968.
[2] R. A. Solo: 'Business enterprise and economic development'. *Michigan State University Business Topics*, Winter 1967, p. 24.

necessary high standards are maintained, which may require some measure of government subsidy. The Management Development and Productivity Centres supported by the ILO in many LDCs have made a useful contribution in this area.

INDUSTRIAL RESEARCH

In an industrializing country, the spectrum of scientific and technical activities can range from fundamental research, through applied research and development, to extension and support services, and into the management and production activities of industry. But in practice neither human nor material resources normally allow more than a partial coverage of these activities and it is essential to establish priorities. While in the early stages heavy reliance must be placed on foreign technology, in the long term, for the full exploitation of the country's material resources, and for the necessary adaptation of imported technology to local materials and conditions, technological research will be required. The rate at which this can be developed will depend on many factors, but particularly the supply of qualified personnel with the right training. But research, like imported technology, is of no value unless it is exploited. Leaving aside the whole question of environmental factors, including the general level of skills in the labour force, availability of finance and so on, the successful application of technology in industry demands, in the first instance, a certain degree of managerial and technical competence at the production level. To the extent to which individual enterprises cannot provide this adequately for themselves, they must be helped from outside, with supporting services. For all these activities, qualified technical staff are required, and optimum overall effectiveness depends on their balanced deployment.

As shown in Chapter I, R and D accounts for only 5–10 per cent of the total costs of a successful innovation. Not all R and D leads to new products and processes, but even allowing for this, total innovative expenditure is likely to be some five times that spent on R and D. In addition to funds, expertise—management as well as technical—will be required throughout the implementation stages. Technical staff are also required for the continual small but cumulatively important cost cutting and operational improvements made at the factory floor level. Within R and D itself, the engineering design and development stages account for the major part of the total effort, and resources should be allocated accordingly. In many LDCs, the research emphasis is on basic scientific work, often of scant relevance to local economic needs, even in the long run, while little attention is paid to strengthening the technical competence of the industrial structure, and its planning and administration, through encouraging qualified personnel—technicians, engineers, technologists—to go into industry, its supporting services, engineering development and applied research.

For various economic and social reasons, in most LDCs, little research is undertaken by or within industry itself, and in the main it has therefore to be both financed and carried out by government organizations. This raises the central questions—how to ensure that R and D is related to actual needs, that the results are commercially exploitable, and that they are in fact beneficially exploited? With a lack of demand pressures relayed from the consumers, and a limited supply of industrialists and entrepreneurs, whether within the private or the public sector, able to recognize opportunities and follow them through to economic exploitation, the problem of research relevance and the application of results requires special attention to institutional arrangements, which have so far been largely neglected.

As a result, though some useful work has been done, the net contribution has been very limited. It has been estimated, for example, that less than 1 per cent of Pakistan's industrial programme has been based on the technological research carried out under the auspices of the Council for Scientific and Industrial Research. In India in 1966–7 the national laboratories under CSIR could realize only Rs 4·53 crore by selling their processes while the total outlay on these laboratories had by that time reached Rs. 146·76 crore.[1]

Without effective relations between research institutes and potential industrial users, the results fail to reach industrial use, there is no useful flow of information, and the research effort is wasted. Linkage may meet problems from either side. Potential research customers may be wealthy industrialists looking for

[1] 'A coherent science policy'. *Yojana*, India, 31 May 1970.

quick safe returns or they may be small-scale low-capital industries—for either, imported technology may have the advantages of less risk, the prestige of an established name, and rapid financial returns, and is therefore considered preferable. Scientists themselves may often bring a monastic environment into applied research laboratories, leading to isolation from the outside world. To bridge these attitudes, careful attention must be paid to the planning, organization, and management of research, its development and sale.

In the environment of a fledgling industry, a research organization is required to do more than research, it must itself take on an entrepreneurial function, and carry an innovation further towards economic exploitation than is normally necessary in a fully industrialized setting. The organization will probably be the main centre of scientific and technological know-how to which the industrialist or entrepreneur can turn. But often the experience and knowledge of the industrialist will be strictly limited and in the application of science and technology in industry the institute must take the initiative. This may require taking a new process through the scaling-up stages, even to a turnkey project. Siddiqui[1] has pointed out that where industry is not developed, research utilization boards involving industrialists may be of little use, and the research groups need to be closely associated with projects all the way through to commercial exploitation.

In an LDC industrial research is needed both to solve day-to-day production problems and to explore the potential for future industrial expansion. Short-term research is important, particularly in the early stages, but should not be allowed to swamp long-term research. As an industry develops, it can be expected to provide at least its short-term service needs increasingly within its own structure, either at the individual firm level or through co-operative research and trade associations, leaving national research organizations to concentrate on longer-term projects.

This trend has been noted, for example, in the U.S.S.R., where in the early stages of industrialization short-term problems and trouble-shooting were dealt with by the Science Academies, but as industry developed and the supply of

---

[1] S. Siddiqui: 'Problems relating to the utilisation of research results'. *Development Digest*, IV, No. 4, January 1967, p. 76.

qualified personnel increased, the trend was towards short-term applied work within industry, long-term applied work in research institutes, and fundamental research in Academies or Universities.

Similarly in Thailand, initially the Applied Scientific Research Corporation and the laboratories of the Ministry of Industry have been concentrating on problems of immediate practical use to existing industries, while at the same time attention was paid to manpower planning, the development of industrial and vocational training, and to various supporting services including a Management Development and Productivity Centre, Standards Institute and so on. In the second phase, which is now being initiated, the Corporation will concentrate on longer-term projects.

A research institute has, then, the responsibility for actively and energetically selling its facilities to potential users, and making sure that industrialists and entrepreneurs remain aware of the services which are available. The first essential is of course that the institute has something to sell—'the practical demonstration of an ability to bring substantial gains to the user must be the chief promotional tool'.[1] The institute needs to keep in constant touch with potential customers, and develop an intimacy with their needs and problems, which requires close liaison at all levels. The capacity of these potential users to take advantage of improved techniques is of evident relevance in assessing the technical and economic practicability of results. Possible applications must be communicated intelligibly and persuasively to the client, not just made available. It is particularly necessary in the case of small-scale industries to ensure that results are presented in a simple and assimilable form.

The recognition of the need to overcome the mutual unintelligibility of industrialists or craftsmen on the one hand and scientists and research workers on the other hand is of vital importance.[2] The organization of technological troubleshooting clinics, technical advisory and consultation services

---

[1] *Manual on the management of industrial research institutes in developing countries.* United Nations, New York, 1966.

[2] Y. Nayudamma: 'Promoting the industrial application of research in an underdeveloped country'. *Minerva*, V, No. 3, Spring 1967, p. 331.

can help to develop communication links. Non-confidential results should be widely disseminated using all available media publications, pictures, films, etc., backed by extension and follow-up work. The process is further helped by frequent meetings between research workers, advisory panels and industrial personnel—all aimed to foster a two-way communication system to teach the latter the use of research as a way to solve problems, and to bring these problems to the attention of the research staff.

An industrial research organization is essentially a source of information to industry, drawing not only on its own research resources but through its expert staff, being able to tap scientific and technological knowledge from any source. The organization thus serves as a discriminating channel for maintaining contact with world science and engineering, actively seeking out, evaluating, and appropriately modifying components of foreign technology. But it can fulfil this role effectively only as an indigenous organization, working with the support and participation of various sections of social and economic life, sensitive to the practical needs and problems of local industry, and identifying itself with the overall economic aspiration of the government and the country.

Though initially the research organization will probably have to be financed entirely by the government, and will require at least government subsidy thereafter, as early as possible industry should be encouraged to sponsor research projects, for a sense of participation and financial involvement. Conversely, some dependence on industrial funding can help to ensure research relevance. Economic incentives can be used at both factory and laboratory levels to stimulate the process of technological innovation. A Russian attitude to this question may be pertinent to LDCs—as summed up by Academician Trapeznikov, that research institutes should be paid by results and that the price system must be the chief lever to encourage the use of new technology.[1]

But at the same time, a research institute needs a reasonable degree of freedom of action, within the framework of the national development plan. In its advisory and consultative

[1] *Science policy in the U.S.S.R.*, OECD, 1969, p. 458.

role it must remain impartial and non-political, performing competently, independently, and without bias.

RESEARCH AND TECHNICAL SERVICES

An industrial research institute then needs to be more than a scientific research organization. It must render various technical services and carry out scientific, engineering, economic, and socio-economic investigations on industrial projects believed to have ultimate practical significance, whether initiated by the research institute, government agencies, individual firms, investors, or industrial associations.

According to the Director of the Indian Central Leather Research Institute, 'the tasks of the research institutes comprise the proper identification and selection of problems in accordance with a ranking of priorities implicit in the choice of these projects relevant to economic growth'.[1] He lists the main objectives of such institutions as:

a) to conduct fundamental and applied research:
b) to develop know-how for better, newer products, processes and uses, better use of indigenous resources, etc.:
c) to disseminate the know-how to industry:
d) to furnish technical consultancy, techno-economic and routine services:
e) to carry out operational studies: and, in some cases,
f) to train technical personnel.

It is interesting to note that a similar range of functions was found necessary in the research institutions set up in the Central Asian Soviet Republics from the 1920s, to help industrial development. According to Duzhenkov,

Applied research plays a key role in promoting industrial development. Its main functions in accelerating development from any level are as follows:

a) to explore and examine the natural wealth and see how it can be developed:
b) to adapt processes to local conditions:
c) to develop new processes for working local materials:
d) to devise methods of obtaining new products and utilising the output:

[1] Y. Nayudamma: op. cit., p. 324.

e) to raise the efficiency of the operating enterprises:
f) to improve quality; to devise suitable methods of quality control:
g) to elaborate adequate siting and development patterns both for separate projects and entire economic areas:
h) to ensure standardisation, provide relevant information, etc.

The relative importance of any of these functions may vary depending on the level of development, the available scientific force and natural resources, and government policy. In the case of the Central Asian Republics each of the functions referred to has come into its own. Each line of research has yielded results of great economic and social significance and sped up industrial development by supplying the answers needed.[1]

An industrial research organization in an LDC is thus required to perform a wide range of functions. An important part of its work will be concerned with surveying local raw materials, and investigating possibilities for their use and development as new products, in improved or entirely new processes, or allowing new uses of existing products. It will also be concerned with quality and productivity improvements and reduced costs in traditional industries. A study of the scientific, and probably economic and social aspects of traditional processes may be necessary to allow an understanding from which improvements can be developed, as for example in leather tanning. The fundamental scientific research carried out by or sponsored by an industrial research organization will stem essentially from these applied problems. But the main focus will be on multi-disciplinary assignments requiring the interaction of science, technology, engineering, economics, and the social sciences. Economic and social studies will need to parallel those in the natural sciences, so that technical findings can be expressed in terms of costs and practical feasibility.

Successful industrialization requires the provision of a whole range of supporting services to augment the technical and managerial competencies of individual enterprises. These services may include technical information and library services; surveys of industrialization possibilities; technological, social, and economic feasibility studies; investment project studies;

[1] V. Duzhenkov: *Science and industrial development. Central Asian Soviet Republics: a practical experience.* U.S.S.R. Academy of Sciences, Moscow, 1967.

pre-project planning; applied scientific research and pilot plant development; market research; layout, organization and productivity improvements; standards and specifications; testing laboratories and quality control; equipment services; technical trouble-shooting; technical and management counselling; and extension services.

In an evolving industry it is vitally important to foster the concept of quality control, for raw materials, intermediaries, and finished products. To this end a standards organization will be required, bringing together representatives of industry, trade, consumer organizations, professional bodies, the scientific and technical community, research organizations, and government. The organization of standards has been described as one of the major co-ordinating factors for orderly economic development on a planned basis.[1] But this can be effective only with knowledgeable industrial participation.

National standards and quality control are particularly important in the promotion of exports, but they can be useful generally in developing industry's level of technology, sometimes feeding problems back to research organizations. Testing laboratories are required—initially perhaps on a centralized basis, but as an industry or an enterprise grows, it will need its own laboratory, from which ultimately its own R and D may develop. Similarly management development and productivity centres, apart from their direct contribution in improving management practices and fostering cost consciousness and efficiency attitudes, can help to identify problems which need the attention of a research organization.

The precise form an organization should take to provide these functions will be conditioned by a number of factors, including the stage of development, the human and material resources, and existing institutions. Any particular institution may cover only a proportion of the activities discussed, but the different functions are often deeply inter-related, and cannot be separated without some loss of effectiveness. Skilled management and technical leadership are rare qualities, and a multiplicity of small dispersed organizations leads to inefficiency and dissipated efforts. On the other hand, as a general principle, the

[1] 'Industrial development and standardisation', prepared for the Athens Symposium, UNIDO, ID/CONF.1/8 of 26 May 1967.

closer the links from R and D through to the production and marketing system the better, particularly at the development engineering and design stages. The physical form which the organization assumes is probably less important than the effectiveness of the communications network which is established to inter-link industry, government, and research.

RESEARCH MANAGEMENT

Overall control of a publicly financed industrial research institute is usually placed in the hands of a government appointed management board. On this board a full perspective of industrial development interests—government, industry, and labour—should be represented, and not solely the scientific and technical community. Particularly where the relationship between government and industry is one of mistrust and lack of mutual confidence, autonomy from government is desirable, though the board may report to an appropriate Minister. Sometimes normal government administrative practices may tend to be inconsistent with the needs of a research institute, which requires long-term continuity in finance, but internal flexibility. Excessive susceptibility to changeable political pressures may produce an atmosphere inimical to good research. Even when largely or entirely dependent on government support, therefore, public accountability of research institutions should not extend to day-to-day control. Given assigned tasks and funds, decision-making at the laboratory level is best decentralized.

A very useful *Manual on the management of industrial research institutes in developing countries* has been prepared under the auspices of the United Nations.[1] As the manual emphasizes, the most important appointment is the Director, who must combine the abilities of both a scientist and an administrator. In some respects the management of research is different from the management of most other activities. Research workers tend to be individualists and need a reasonable degree of freedom from detailed supervision in carrying out their work. An atmosphere free from rigid controls and disciplinary restrictions is required,

[1] Op. cit.

and management is rather an enabling process,[1] providing the money and facilities, the right climate for research and the implementation of results. Good management stimulates creativity—individual creativity is the cornerstone of research productivity, and the success of the research organization depends on combining the creativity of many people. The art of research management is to weld creative individual initiatives into a concerted team effort. To this end the internal organization structure needs to be flexible, and tailored to suit the nature of the work and the abilities and personalities of the individual staff members. Good research cannot be expected if morale is low. While the main motivation of scientists stems from the nature of their work, fair personnel practices, including reasonable promotion prospects and remuneration, are also important.

As a key figure in the communications network with industry and government, the Director must have time to maintain outside contacts and to plan the work of the institute. This implies adequate staff assistance, but in practice he is often overloaded with administrative responsibilities, and not given enough opportunities to delegate authority. Other defects have been reported:

Outmoded organizations, autocratically-made decisions, improper planning, emphasis on prestige and on newsworthy projects, lack of congenial working conditions, gerontocracy, and the discouragement of initiative among younger staff members are some of the factors which militate against effective research. Where one or more of these factors is present, a drastic change is called for.[2]

Mrs. Gandhi, addressing the Indian Science Congress, has noted that

Many scientists feel frustrated. Research institutions suffer from lack of flexibility. Certain tasks cannot be carried out owing to 'procedural' difficulties. There are also unnecessary irritations from the interference of the bureaucracy at headquarters. We are not getting all the returns possible from our investments in scientific

[1] E. S. Hiscocks: 'The organisation of industrial research in developing countries'. Prepared as a background document for the Athens Symposium, UNIDO, ID/CONF.1/B.14, of 15 May 1967.
[2] Y. Nayudamma: op. cit., p. 326.

research. Nor are we utilising the talents of our young people in the best manner.[1]

Management has a responsibility for the systematic development of younger men, offering them opportunities to extend their abilities and graduate into other positions. For most research workers, their creativity reaches a peak at a relatively early age and then declines. In physical sciences, for example, it has been suggested that the peak is normally between 30 and 35 years. To make full use of the experience and knowledge of older research workers, the career structure should not be based on a life-time in research, except for those few who retain their inventiveness and become research leaders. For the majority, arrangements should be made to absorb older research workers into other areas, such as administration, production control, or technical sales, where their experience can be useful, leaving room for a continual inflow of younger researchers. In this way, research institutes can be useful training centres for industry.

Appropriate support ratios of professional research staff to technical assistants vary considerably between fields, and between bench research and engineering development, but usually average about three technicians per researcher. A lack of middle-level technicians is often a serious bottleneck in LDCs, and without them research productivity is likely to be low.

Even small research units require access to workshop facilities, such as metal working or glass blowing. With larger organizations, more specialized workshops may be needed, possibly including design and engineering facilities. The industrial application of R and D results often demands the design and construction of equipment and machinery, and a large research organization should have a drawing office and facilities for design, testing, and inspection. Instrument maintenance and repair is another important field which may be decisive in research productivity.

CHOICE OF TECHNIQUES

A basic aim in economic development is increased productivity —more or better goods and services from the available resources.

[1] 'Role of science in a developing society'—Excerpts from an address by Prime Minister Indira Gandhi, *Indian and Foreign Review*, 7, No. 8, 1970.

The overall aspect of productivity needs to be distinguished from that of labour productivity, which is but one of its components and not necessarily the one most in need of improvement. In improving overall productivity it seems logical to concentrate first on the vital resources in limited supply.

Most industrial technologies in current use derive from developed countries, and have been designed to suit their conditions—high-cost and scarce labour, adequate supplies of capital, technical and managerial skills, relatively large high-income markets, virtual full employment. Large markets offer opportunities to take advantage of economies of scale, and there is strong pressure to economize on labour as a means to increased productivity.

In LDCs the situation is of course very different, capital and skills are in limited supply, but often there is an abundance of unskilled labour, and a high level of unemployment and under-employment. Domestic markets tend to be small, with low purchasing power. Without wider external markets, these countries cannot normally take full advantage of economies of scale.

If a prime aim in LDCs is to make the most effective use of the resources in limited supply—particularly capital and foreign exchange, then, in contrast to the developed countries, the most appropriate technologies are 'capital-saving'. In most cases these may involve employing relatively more people—but this is not necessarily so. However, quite apart from the human and moral aspects of the problem, it would be wasteful not to make the fullest possible use of the available labour potential. In fact, with the rapid rate of population growth unemployment is rising. David Morse, the former Director-General of the ILO has estimated[1] that to absorb both the projected increase in the labour force and the existing visible surplus of labour supply, around 300 million jobs will have to be created in LDCs between now and 1980. This will not be possible without a broader range of more appropriate or intermediate technologies which will allow useful employment at minimum capital cost.

It cannot be expected therefore that the labour-saving, capital-intensive technologies of the advanced countries will be

[1] D. Morse: 'Dimensions of the employment problem in developing countries'. Keynote paper at the Cambridge Conference on Development, 1970.

10

well suited to the needs of LDCs. With these technologies, rapid economic growth and increased employment in LDCs may be incompatible. In some countries a relatively high rate of economic growth has been accompanied by a decrease in the level of employment. This conflict seems inevitable unless equally efficient capital-saving, labour-intensive technologies can be devised and are adopted.

In some industries, the possibilities for substituting labour for capital are restricted, because of quality requirements or operating conditions. Furthermore, though modern techniques often require more capital, and absorb less manpower, in many cases LDCs are virtually compelled to use them because they are more efficient in the economic sense, i.e. they increase the amount of product obtainable per unit of capital.[1] Capital-intensive equipment may be the only type available, and LDCs must either buy this or pay a higher price for special equipment designed to suit their conditions. With many key processes, such as steel or fertilizer manufacture, both capital and operating costs fall rapidly with increasing plant size, and large-scale production units are probably inevitable (though even here modern technological developments often tend to lower the minimum scale for efficient operation). Despite the investment involved, the lower unit costs are not always realized in LDCs, as economies of scale in such plants can be readily dissipated by working well below capacity, or by an excessive diversification of product.

Various other factors can lead to a tendency towards the selection of capital-intensive methods at the business enterprise level. A shortage of supervisors may argue against labour-intensive techniques. While unskilled labour can only rarely be a direct substitute for capital, managerial or technical skills can more frequently replace capital, and possibly can be more easily acquired than capital. Managerial skills are in any case of vital importance in the efficient use of existing capital resources—better use of an existing plant may avoid or defer the need to invest in a second. Management's choice of technology may be affected by market distortions of the prices of labour and capital. In practice, through a variety of causes, interest rates may not reflect the scarcity of capital, while wage

[1] ECLA: op. cit., p. 83.

rates may not reflect a position of labour abundance. Decisions made by firms on the basis of the actual prices they pay for machines and labour may not necessarily be the most advantageous to society as a whole. Governments can help to reduce such discrepancies through their fiscal and tax policies. But even if the distortions were rectified, there would still be a need to make available a fuller spectrum of techniques which can operate efficiently under the constraints of economic conditions, manpower resources, distribution and marketing conditions of LDCs.

This does not necessarily mean small-scale or primitive techniques. Improved hand tools do have a place in improving productivity. Provided adequate organizational and managerial abilities can be made available, most LDCs have opportunities for extensive projects, such as roads and dams, which can be reasonably based mainly on human labour and simple tools. But very simple technologies can be an economic trap—even at subsistence wages manpower harnessed to a machine costs about $1 per kWh, while small diesel units even in high cost areas can produce at about 20 cts. per kWh.[1] At the other end of the spectrum the use of computers may be appropriate technology, as in stock control to reduce the capital cost of inventories.

Much more research is needed on the range of technology substitutions which are possible. As noted above, in some areas modern technological developments are tending to reduce the minimum scale of economic operation and research specifically aimed in this direction could well be fruitful. Efficient low-capital small-market units should be feasible in many fields. Sometimes, more detailed engineering design can provide a substitute for considerable amounts of capital. While the choice of a central production process may be restricted, less capital-intensive techniques can be used in auxiliary operations such as materials handling. The application of science and technology can radically improve the productivity of traditional processes, based on empirical techniques.

The urgent need is for large-scale opportunities to manufacture products with significant value added using labour-intensive methods. Transistor radios and fibreglass car bodies

[1] J. E. Stepanek: 'An engineer scans the developing world'. Olin Lectures, Yale University, 1969, p. 13.

are examples of technologically advanced industries of this sort. More traditional labour-intensive industries such as leather, textiles or printing could also offer opportunities to take advantage of present wage differentials, if more liberal trade policies towards these goods were adopted in developed countries. Joint manufacturing programmes may be useful, with the more labour-intensive operations being carried out in LDCs, though this may smack of economic colonialism. For example, clothes cut in the U.S. are sent to Latin American countries for stitching and finishing for the U.S. market.[1] India's exports of automobile components have increased from Rs. 3·8 M. in 1968/69 to Rs. 9 M. in 1969/70.[2]

The major short-term contribution to increased employment will have to come from agriculture, which for many years is likely to depend a great deal on human and animal power, though in some areas specifically designed items such as Ford's two-wheeled DNT tractor with 'a price roughly comparable to a pair of oxen' may have considerable relevance. Agricultural development can lead to a large increase in demand for relatively simple inexpensive farm equipment suited to local manufacture in rural workshops, using capital-saving, labour-intensive techniques. Improved agricultural implements are often restricted by a lack of technical skills, such as blacksmiths, wheelwrights, and rural mechanics. Systematic programmes are needed to design and test appropriate equipment, with extension and training services to promote rural industrial development and small-scale industries.

Both Japan and China offer examples of countries which have deliberately followed courses of technological pluralism. Japan has made extensive use of labour-saving techniques in many manufacturing sectors. At an earlier stage of development, major capital-intensive industries were served by a large number of small labour-intensive shops, where much lower wage rates were paid. But such a system requires a high level of managerial ability, plus a social discipline which allows wage discrepancies to be remedied in pace with economic growth.

---

[1] G. Chandler: 'The effect of the flow of private sector finance on employment in less developed countries'. Background paper, Cambridge Conference on Development, 1970.

[2] *Far East Trade and Development*, 25, No. 9, September 1970, p. 437.

China[1] is attempting the simultaneous development of techniques with varying degrees of mechanization, including technologically simple industries to mobilize local resources despite the national constraints of materials shortages, transport and storage bottlenecks, and seasonal labour requirements in agriculture.

One of the more active organizations in this area is the Intermediate Technology Development Group, based in London, which serves as a clearing house for information, and also promotes applied research in such fields as building, water supply, rural health, and agriculture. The Group works in association with various official and non-official bodies in countries such as India, Ghana, Nigeria, Tanzania, Kenya, and Zambia, and has collaborated with a number of U.N. agencies. With financial support from both private and official sources, some £100,000 in project funds have been allocated. Such efforts would seem to merit very much more vigorous support.

---

[1] C. Riskin: 'Local industry and choice of techniques in planning of industrial development in mainland China'. *Planning for Advanced Skills and Technologies*, UNIDO, Vienna, 1968, p. 171.

V   Education and Manpower

INTRODUCTION

Free and universal education is now accepted as a basic human right, at least in principle. In LDCs widespread expansion of general education has been seen as a symbol of hope for the future—for the nation and for the individual. Governments have been faced with strong popular demand for equal educational opportunities for all, and enormous efforts have been made to expand educational systems, particularly at the primary level. Total enrolments in schools and universities in LDCs almost tripled between 1950 and 1965. As expressed by the Pearson Commission, while there may be doubts about the efficiency of educational systems in certain developing countries, 'there is no doubt that the growth of educational opportunities has been dramatic and has broadened the horizons of millions of people'.[1] And this, of course, is fundamental to the development process.

Inevitably these achievements have been very costly. LDCs are now spending on average 5 per cent of their national income on education. This expenditure is not aimed primarily towards economic growth but to meet a wide range of social, cultural, and political objectives, though these are naturally not unrelated to economic development, as for example in the general reduction of illiteracy. Satisfaction of the social demand for education is a necessary part of any education programme, but the resources of LDCs are limited, and some educational priority needs to be given to meeting specific manpower needs. But to quote the Pearson Commission again, 'educational systems are not generally designed to produce intermediate skills or proficiencies that correspond to the needs of industry, agriculture, or government in the less developed countries'.[2] Often, their educational systems fail to provide either a satis-

---

[1] *Partners in Development.* Report of the Pearson Commission, 1969, p. 43.
[2] Ibid., p. 68.

factory general education or a level of skill in the labour force appropriate to the needs of the country.

Certainly, heavy expenditure on education does not offer an automatic solution to skill shortages. Education may be too academic and bear little relation to practical needs. Primary and secondary training is usually designed as preparation for a higher level of education, which most pupils will never reach.[1] At University level, status subjects such as law may predominate over technical subjects. For example, in India 23 per cent, and in Uruguay only 6 per cent of university students were studying in fields related to science or technology. Though the vast majority of the people depend on agriculture for their livelihood, and at least adaptive research on agriculture and natural resources must necessarily be done locally, only about 5 per cent of university students in LDCs are in agriculture or cognate subjects, and relatively little research is being undertaken into the social, political, and economic problems of rural development. The wrong sort of education, or an imbalance between different subjects and levels can be more wasteful of human and economic resources than too little education.

MANPOWER PLANNING AND EDUCATION

Planning at government level is becoming increasingly important, as highly sensitive political decisions have to be made. With the limited resources available some attempt has to be made to establish priorities, to keep targets within practical limits, improve the effectiveness of education and make training better adapted to employment.[2] But while the effective coupling of education with the system of employment generation and the utilization of human resources remains a high priority, it must be recognized that much more needs to be known about the relationship between the occupational structure and the education system before the most appropriate educational profile can be defined.

[1] *Development and utilisation of human resources in developing countries.* Report of the Secretary-General, U.N. Economic and Social Council, E/4353, 8 May 1967, p. 21.
[2] OECD: *Problems of Human Resources Planning in Latin America and in the Mediterranean Regional Project Countries.* 1965.

The methodology of relating manpower needs and the education system is far from accurate. In theory manpower plans stem from national goals, but the decisions which determine actual skill requirements are made at many levels, and planning can therefore be only approximate—though it may help to channel resources towards producing the type of manpower required. In many countries, manpower planning is inevitably somewhat rudimentary, given the lack of reliable data, the uncertainties of development plans, inadequate administrative expertise, and the absence of centralized controls. In practice, it seems doubtful whether anyone really knows how to integrate educational into general planning in a mixed economy,[1] and even if it were theoretically possible, with the popular demand for education the results might not be politically feasible.

Economic and educational growth do not necessarily follow parallel trends. Though growth may be impossible without education, by itself education does not create economic growth. Already it has been reported[2] that in most Latin American countries the output of primary school teachers exceeds the absorption capacity of the labour market, and an excess of graduates is likely in the long run. In some countries the higher education system is already producing more college graduates than the economy can absorb at levels which could justify the cost of their training, as for example in the Philippines and parts of India—the era of college-educated unemployables has started.[3] Quite apart from the question of how appropriate the education may be, the pressure for education seems likely to lead to an inevitable lag between the output of the education system and the capacity of the society to absorb them.

But further, as a consequence of the high rate of population growth in LDCs, the problem of school leavers is rapidly becoming equated with the general problem of unemployment. In this context the crucial question is, as stressed by the Vice-Chancellor of the Jawaharlal Nehru University in New

---

[1] C. A. Anderson and P. Foster: 'Middle Africa in the 1980's: the Outlook for Education'. Symposium on *Africa in the 1970's and 80's. Issues in Development* organized by the Adlai Stevenson Institute of International Affairs, Chicago, 1968. Frederick S. Arkhurst (ed.), Praeger, 1970.

[2] OECD, op. cit., p. 48.

[3] G. Hunter: *Modernizing Peasant Societies*, op. cit., p. 240.

Delhi:[1] trained and educated for what? 'Educated unemployment can be effectively tackled only by vocationalising education and making it job-oriented at the lower and middle levels.' The Vice-Chancellor notes that in India the engineer-technician ratio is 1:1·4, with plans to increase this to 1:3 by 1986, while in the U.K., for example, the recommended ratio is 1:5. Similarly, Arthur Lewis has remarked[2] that while the few university trained persons who are needed in LDCs can, at a pinch, be imported, five to ten times as many secondary school products are needed. 'Secondary school products are the steel framework of the economy—as technicians, record-keepers, supervisors, teachers, managers, and administrators.'

As Lord Blackett has pointed out,[3] educational strategy should reflect to some extent the relative importance, in the long and short term, of the main sources of material wealth—mineral resources, including oil and natural gas; agricultural production, including forestry and fisheries; industry; and in some cases tourism. For each of these sectors the educational needs will be different, though all will require good administrators and managers.

The exploitation of mineral resources does not normally involve large numbers of trained people, but does require some highly specialized personnel—geologists, geophysicists, geo-chemists, mining engineers, and extraction metallurgists. The considerable capital costs which are entailed in most mineral developments often make outside assistance essential, usually in the form of a specialist international corporation, which will have its own expert staff. But technical training of local people working within these organizations can be important, and the development of indigenous specialists deserves a higher priority than is normally given.

For most LDCs, agriculture, forestry, and fisheries account for a considerable part of the national income, and involve a substantial proportion of the population. Modernization of

[1] G. Parthasarathi: 'Education and Social Progress'. Fourth Annual Tagore Lecture, *India News*, 17 October 1970.

[2] W. A. Lewis: *The Development Process*. Executive Briefing Paper, No. 2, United Nations Centre for Economic and Social Information, 1970.

[3] Lord Blackett: *Reflexions on Science and Technology in Developing Countries*. Gandhi Memorial Lectures, East African Publishing House, Nairobi, January 1969, I, p. 14.

agriculture and the adoption of new technologies will require widespread rural education and a literate peasantry. Large numbers of extension workers and technicians are also needed, backed by specialists in environmental studies and adaptive research. These are not likely to be forthcoming unless agriculture can become a dynamic sector, which offers careers as attractive and remunerative as those in industry.

The educational needs of manufacturing industry will become increasingly complex and varied, as the industrial structure becomes more sophisticated. Development calls for a wide range of skills, and most LDCs require an expansion of vocational and technical education, to correct the imbalance in the training and distribution of technical personnel. For economic growth the real need from the education system is likely to be the production of large numbers of technicians, smaller numbers of technologists, and a reasonable supply of technologically-minded managers and entrepreneurs.[1]

Education costs tend to be high, particularly in Africa. The ratio of costs per pupil between higher education and primary schooling in Africa is often as high as 30:1, compared with 5:1 in Canada or Australia. Though this high ratio may be attributable in part to the necessity in African universities to provide residential accommodation for students and to the high cost of expatriate staff, there does seem scope to improve efficiency—both in terms of cost efficiency, through reducing unit costs, as by better training procedures and wider or multiple use of facilities, and more general economic efficiency in the sense of using resources only when their benefits exceed their costs. But a major problem in such analyses is the clear definition of output and its quality in the context of education, which may require considerable educational research. Various modern management techniques for comparing output with education costs, essentially modified forms of cost effectiveness analysis, such as Programme Planning and Budgeting System (PPBS) in the U.S.A., and Output Budgeting in the U.K., have shown some promise. These techniques are still under development, but as suggested at a recent OECD meeting,[2] they can make an

[1] Lord Todd: House of Lords Official Report, 4 March 1970, p. 411.
[2] OECD: 'Conference on policies for educational growth—Conclusions', June 1970.

invaluable contribution to improved resource allocation by helping to bring about:

(a) more rigorous formulation of goals,
(b) examination of unit costs,
(c) comparisons of costs and benefits of different programmes.

NEW APPROACHES TO SCIENCE TEACHING

As Homi Bhabha, the late Director of the Tata Institute of Fundamental Science in India, once said: 'The problem of establishing science as a live and vital force in society is an inseparable part of the problem of transforming an industrially under-developed to a developed country.'[1] Development and social change cannot be achieved without building up a certain minimum of scientific culture. LDCs need to foster a wider and deeper understanding of scientific methods and their applications, both at the adult level, through adult education programmes and the use of mass communications media, and in the normal educational system. Science must form an essential part of general education, as a means for developing the attitudes of critical inquiry, adaptability and objective understanding. The earlier this educational process starts the better.

Compared with those in developed countries, children in LDCs are not exposed in daily life to continual contact with examples of applied science and technology, and are less likely to be encouraged to ask questions and to develop an inquiring attitude of mind. Predominantly the school has, therefore, to form their outlook and provide the experiences which tend to a much greater extent to be inherent in the environment in an advanced industrialized society.[2] Not only should science be taught at the secondary school level, but scientific and technical education should start much earlier, with the help of scientific toys and hand tools. For most children, primary school represents the only formal education they will receive, and the level of scientific literacy of the future adult population depends largely on what they learn there.

[1] H. J. Bhabha: 'Science and the Problems of Development'. *ICSU Bulletin*, March 1966, p. 26.
[2] UNESCO: *An Asian Model of Educational Development*, 1966, p. 108.

Science introduced at lower educational levels is not to be regarded as skill training, but should provide the foundation for an objective, experimental approach to the environment, and some understanding of scientific method. Children must be given an appreciation of cause and effect in daily life, to replace the essentially non-scientific assumptions sometimes involved in traditional cultural explanations of natural phenomena. Traditional methods of education, with an emphasis on teaching by rote-learning, often based on outdated texts, cannot achieve these aims. Modern science education attempts to treat science not as an accumulation of facts but as an experience in investigation and discovery, and aims to stimulate an inquiring and analytical mind.

Radically new approaches to the teaching of science and maths have been developed in advanced countries during recent years, and LDCs can take advantage of the thinking behind these new methods, while adapting the content to suit their particular circumstances. Wherever possible the process of science should be taught using relevant materials as the vehicle. Some notable examples of adaptation have already taken place, but much remains to be done. These problems have been discussed recently at a conference on Science and Education in Developing States held at Rehovot, Israel, in August, 1969. It was concluded that most of what children need to know can be put into a clearly relevant context: 'The scientific study of soils, of mosquitoes and flies, of rainfall and sunshine, or animal behaviour are all examples of contexts which are directly and obviously relevant to national goals and priorities, and yet provide ample scope for the introduction and exploration of scientific ways of thinking.'[1] Some experimental facilities will be essential, but simple equipment is often more helpful for the comprehension of fundamental concepts than expensive, complex apparatus. Improvisation using the resources of the environment may be better suited to activity-oriented teaching methods, and teachers need to be shown how to set up simple experiments.[2] Many teachers, especially at

[1] J. S. Goldstein: 'Special Opportunities for Science Teaching in Developing Countries'. From *Science and Education in Developing States*, Proceedings of the Fifth Rehovot Conference, Philip and Hadassah Gillon (eds.), Praeger, 1971.
[2] UNESCO: op. cit., p. 110.

primary level, have little or no science background, and need systematic in-service training to prepare them to handle the new materials and approaches.

To combine quantitative expansion of science education with qualitative improvement, within the financial limitation of LDCs, will require radical innovations. Reforms must be introduced and continually adapted, as part of an overall adaptation of the educational system to meet the needs of modern times, and prepare young people for future society. But education is often even more resistant to innovation than industry.[1] In some cases education does not readily assume its proper role as an instrument of social reform, because of the codification of school curricula, centralized management, overcrowded classrooms, stereotyped examinations, and the general rigidity of the teaching profession. Unfortunately, some teachers are quite happy with the old system under which they themselves were taught, and are 'rusted in syllabusitis'.[2] Where these problems arise teachers training colleges have a key role in improvement.

The systematic introduction of innovation into educational planning and reform is likely to require extensive fundamental and applied research in education, including pilot projects and their scientific evaluation, and supervised implementation. Full curricula revision may require a national centre where educationalists and scientists can work together, as for example the Science Education Centre at the University of the Philippines, designed to promote educational research, and to improve teachers' training and teaching aids. Similar national centres have been established in several countries, such as Kenya, Thailand, Brazil, and Israel. There is scope for regional co-operation in this field, too, as demonstrated in the Asian Centre for Education in Sciences and Mathematics at Penang, Malaysia.

SECONDARY AND VOCATIONAL EDUCATION

One of the major weaknesses at secondary level is the narrow academic training which prepares the bulk of the pupils for

[1] OECD: *Human Resources Planning in Latin America.* Op. cit., p. 52.
[2] J. Elstgeest: 'Science Education in the General Teachers' College'. Rehovot Conference on Science and Education in Developing States, op. cit.

universities, to which relatively few will go. It is now generally recognized that secondary education must be redesigned as a terminal point for the many rather than university preparation for the few, with an emphasis on providing the knowledge, skills, and attitudes more appropriate to the needs at work and in life.

In a context of rapid technological change, the skills most needed are adaptability and flexibility. Specific skills may become obsolete very quickly, so that further training and re-training may be necessary. This suggests the importance of a sound initial basic training. Any expansion of vocational and technical education at secondary levels upwards should therefore remain linked with general education, and must include a strong grounding in science and maths. This may require the development of some form of comprehensive schooling, designed primarily to produce technically trained practical people with a broad education. In Iran, for example, academic lower secondary education is being replaced by a 'guidance cycle' designed to stimulate an interest in the practical arts and to channel students into vocational-technical schools and into comprehensive upper secondary schools.

A most important need for most LDCs is a wider range of technical and vocational training at secondary and post-secondary levels, related to rural development. But relatively little is known about the numbers and kinds of trained people needed for rural development, which requires an integrated effort across a very broad front. Various experimental approaches such as the series of pilot projects in Kenya, which include village polytechnics for training related not only to agriculture but to processing and allied industries and services, and the successful Comilla project in East Pakistan, can give useful guidelines, but every country will need to assess the specific needs of each region to suit its stage of development. Formal courses should be paralleled by informal training at voluntary organizations such as Young Farmers' Clubs. The urgency of this problem of training for rural development has been stressed in the FAO's Provisional Indicative World Plan: 'If a considerable programme of expansion of training facilities were *not* to be launched as a matter of high priority, particularly at the intermediate level, only seventeen out of the fifty countries for which data on training facilities were available would meet calculated requirements by 1975, and only fourteen by 1985.'[1]

Vocational training centres for industry have often been criticized for the poor quality of their product—partly from a failure to identify local needs correctly, and partly from an over-theoretical bias. Effective co-ordination between sources of employment and the training system, with suitable feed-back mechanisms, is vitally important. Opportunities for access to practical training at the centres are usually limited, and in-plant training within industry should be encouraged, if necessary with financial incentives. Some combination of on-the-job training, interspersed with a series of short formal courses, may be better suited to the circumstances.

The possibilities for rapid expansion are shown by Singapore, where the number of pupils taking some form of technical training at secondary level increased seven-fold between March 1968, and March 1969. The critical element in this operation has been the teacher retraining programme.[2]

UNIVERSITIES AND HIGHER EDUCATION

The aspiration to establish a full range of university education as early as possible is, understandably, a common feature of all LDCs. But the full benefits of higher education are not likely to be gained unless the system is adapted in form and content to suit the specific cultural, social, and economic environment. To an extent there may be some incompatibility between aiming for general academic standards which match the highest international levels, and making an immediate contribution to development. Sir Eric Ashby[3] has stressed the importance of distinguishing between the quality of teaching in higher education, which should be as high as is practically possible, and standards, which must be set at appropriate levels of attainment which will vary with time and place. As he quotes, there is a danger in accepting 'a quasi-mystical concept of high

[1] FAO: *Provisional Indicative World Plan for Agricultural Development—Summary and Main Conclusions*, Rome, 1970.

[2] R. Greenough: UNESCO and education in Asia. *UNESCO Chronicle*, January 1970, p. 9.

[3] Sir Eric Ashby: *Universities: British, Indian, African*. Weidenfeld & Nicholson, 1966.

standards, which often possess a narrowness directly propor-
tional to their so-called height'. While a narrow approach may
be appropriate in certain fields and in particular institutions,
LDCs seem likely to require a system of higher education which
covers a broad spectrum of studies and standards.

For the effective application of modern technology, trained
scientists, technologists, and engineers are required throughout
the production system, whether industry, agriculture, or
mining, in a wide range of jobs, including administration, design, production, sales, extension, and applied research. They
are also required in the government administrative service and
in the education system. Thus the role of scientists as basic
research workers is but a minor part compared with their
possible contribution to the country's economic growth in other
ways. This emphasizes the importance for most scientists of a
general education which is technologically-oriented rather than
a very highly specialized one.[1] The higher education system
should be so designed as to produce an adequate number of
people with a reasonable degree of practical competence in
agriculture, engineering, and various other technologies, and a
much smaller number of highly competent specialists.

The limited output of scientists and engineers, in comparison
with the advanced countries, is shown in Table 5. Even within
science and technology, in some areas the preference tends to be
heavily in favour of pure science, instead of the vitally needed
technologies. Despite the great strides that have been made in
almost all countries an expansion of advanced training is
urgently needed in science, technology, and engineering, and
also in management, business methods, and economics.

The most serious deficiency is usually in the agricultural
sciences, as indicated in Table 6, though here again there have
been remarkable achievements. In India, for example, university enrolments in agriculture, though still low for an essentially
agricultural community, were increased nearly ten-fold
between 1950 and 1966.[2] In Latin America, the number of
agricultural graduates has been tripled in ten years.[3] But there

---

[1] Lord Blackett: op. cit., II, p. 22.
[2] G. Parthasarathi: op. cit.
[3] O. Olcese: 'Latin America: University education in agriculture'. *Span*, 13,
No. 2, 1970.

TABLE 5
EDUCATION AT THE THIRD LEVEL[a] IN SCIENCE AND TECHNOLOGY—NUMBER OF STUDENTS GRADUATING AROUND 1967

Region	No. of countries	Graduates					No. per 100,000 population		
		Total	Natural sciences	% Total	Engineering	% Total	Total	Natural sciences	Engineering
Africa, excluding Arab States	20	12,115	1,823	15·0	553	4·6	7	1	0·3
Asia[b], excluding Arab States	19	691,714	68,487	9·9	70,548	10·2	75	7	8
of which India[c]		(245,482)	(44,861)	(18·3)	(10,253)	(4·2)	52	10	2
Arab States	11	42,244	3,210	7·6	4,500	10·7	42	3	4
Latin America	23	80,976	2,771	3·4	8,417	10·4	36	1	4
Europe, North America, Oceania, U.S.S.R.	31	1,472,064	167,176	11·4	146,821	10·0	220	25	22
of which U.S.A.		(908,054)	(89,190)	(9·8)	(52,448)	(5·8)	461	45	27
Total	104	2,299,113	243,467	10·6	230,839	10·0	110	12	11

[a] The figures, in general, relate to all kinds of degrees, and diplomas (except honorary degrees)—pre-university, university, post-graduate and non-university.
[b] Not including China (Mainland).
[c] 1964.

Source: Contribution of UNESCO to Stage II of the World Plan of action for the application of science and technology to development.
Reference: SC/WS/93. Paris, 31 July 1970.

TABLE 6

NUMBER OF AGRICULTURAL STUDENTS BY REGION IN RELATION TO THE
STUDENT BODY IN ALL FACULTIES AND TOTAL POPULATION

Region	Total number of students (all faculties) x 1000	Agricultural students x 1000	Agricultural students as % of all students	No. of agricultural students per million pop.
Africa	298	27	9·0	89
Latin America	897	36	4·0	146
Asia (excluding India, China and Japan)	1,387	54	3·9	88
India	1,270	27	2·1	57
Japan	1,150	45	3·9	455
Europe (excluding U.S.S.R.)	3,135	121	3·9	270

Source: Based on data in the *UNESCO Statistical Year Book, 1968*. Given the variations between national systems, and problems of definition, the data can be regarded as indicative only.

are still problems of quality, as well as quantity. Given the dependence of most LDCs on the effective use of biological natural resources, through agriculture, fisheries, forestry, and in some countries wild life and tourism, together with the supporting industries which provide the necessary inputs such as fertilizers, or process the products, it might be expected that activities in these fields should form a central focus in universities to which a wide range of other activities in the humanities and in social and natural sciences are consciously and constructively related.[1] But often agriculture and allied subjects are given a peripheral, low-status position. There is an urgent need to upgrade the status of agriculture and related faculties, and offer incentives to students to enter these courses. In many countries, mineral resources also represent a major source of foreign exchange earnings, but university facilities related to the earth sciences are generally neglected.

A much greater diversity of training in universities or other institutions of higher learning is probably needed in most countries. It is interesting to note that in the U.S.S.R., the universities account for only about 10 per cent of all Soviet students in higher education, and are broadly concerned with the training of the next generation of research workers in arts

[1] A. H. Bunting: personal communication.

and in pure science. The great majority of students attend
institutions which specialize in particular vocational courses,
though the curriculum normally includes general academic
studies. The rapid expansion of Soviet higher education in
recent years has been brought about by a great extension of
evening classes and correspondence courses; particularly for
technological studies.[1]

In the larger LDCs the spectrum of higher education and
training needs will be met by a number of separate institutions—including agricultural colleges, and polytechnics, as well
as universities. But in smaller countries, to conserve resources a
wide range of education may have to be provided within a
single institution. The University of Malawi, for example,
brings together in one academic organization all the higher
levels of post-secondary education in the country, including a
college of agriculture, a college of education, an institute of
public administration, a polytechnic and the more usual
university courses. The value of such an amalgamation in an
LDC can also be argued on other grounds.

The incorporation of all levels of further education into a single
institution differs widely from the common concept of the functions
of a university in many countries, but both the Malawi government
and the university authorities are convinced that only in this way
can the most effective contribution be made to the advancement of
the national economy. In a developing country it is important that a
university should become an integral part of the life of the community and avoid the danger of intellectual isolation. It must also
make the best possible use of its own and the country's potential in
human and material resources. In the interests of economy and
efficiency the present organisation will allow: interchange of staff,
equipment and teaching accommodation; adjustment of courses to
meet the country's changing needs in the output of trained manpower; transfer of students from one course to another as their skills
and capacities are more accurately assessed; and maintenance of
academic, professional and technical standards through the exercise
of a single authority.[2]

At the level of higher scientific education, LDCs present a

[1] A. Nove and J. A. Newth: *The Soviet Middle East*. Allen & Unwin, London,
1967, p. 80.
[2] *Commonwealth Universities Yearbook, 1968*.

wide range of contrasts—from countries with institutions which have earned international reputations as centres of first quality scientific education and research, to countries where higher science education scarcely exists. Though Bolivia, for example, has seven universities, not one has a science faculty. Often science faculties exist largely in name only, with totally inadequate staff and equipment. In some universities there is little or no research, not so much as a matter of policy, but because of the very heavy teaching loads, the poor pay which obliges staff to work part-time elsewhere to gain adequate remuneration, and excessive time spent on routine administrative chores. When research is undertaken it often has little relevance to local problems. Policy and teaching may be in the hands of an academic staff which has become totally outdated not only in specialized knowledge but in general outlook. Some institutions of higher learning in India, for example, have been described as assembly lines for the mass production of graduates and post-graduates of incredibly low quality.[1] More generally, it has been said that 'A large proportion of the world's academies have shrunk to become self-perpetuating centres of scientific "eliteism"; only in a few cases are they sensibly contributing to national decision-making and preparing for the new situation.'[2]

At the undergraduate level it is debatable whether direct research involvement is essential to maintain the quality of teaching—it may be more useful to build up close linkages with existing research. Until recent years the universities in the U.S.S.R. were purely concerned with teaching but they maintained close contacts with the research academies. In LDCs the main research centres are likely to be government establishments, and some degree of integration with university departments may offer the best way to mobilize to the fullest extent all available scientific resources and ensure their best deployment.[3]

[1] A. Parthasarathi: 'Universities and Nation Building'. *Quest*, No. 52, January/March 1967, p. 23.

[2] Alexander King: 'Science policy, economic growth and the quality of life'. Text of the Sixth Annual Science of Science Foundation Lecture, *Science Policy News*, 2, No. 1, July 1970.

[3] Report of the Working Party on Liaison between Universities and Government Research Establishments. Council for Scientific Policy, HMSO Command 3222, 1967.

Closer contacts with industry generally are desirable, reinforced through enlisting the help of technical personnel from industry to contribute to courses, and through the use of university consultants, provided this does not become so extensive as to weaken the university's principal function of education.

But in most LDCs there is an understandable trend towards building up post-graduate training programmes. These can be very expensive, and a rigorously selective approach is essential. Governments and universities need to determine the post-graduate fields which are most relevant to development, and establish priorities taking into account other educational and non-educational investment opportunities. Sending graduates for further training overseas may run the risks of the 'brain drain' and of inappropriate training, but these risks have to be assessed in each particular case, with due regard to costs and local needs.

For effective post-graduate teaching research is virtually essential, but the emphasis can still be on problems which are related to the local environment and natural resources. University scientific research often tends to have a bias towards pure science. In part this may be because pure scientific research is easier to get started, and is little influenced by any considerations outside pure science itself. Furthermore, there is no doubt that basic science is one of the most exciting and intellectually stimulating activities of mankind. But there is a danger of basic scientists withdrawing from the practical world and becoming a lonely *élite* in their own country.

The conditions for effective applied science are quite different. For here the problems studied must be formulated in relation to some practical need recognised by the outside world and the results when obtained must be sold to the outside world. This involves the applied scientist being in close personal contact with his country's industry, agriculture, mining or medicine. So, to select useful projects is often a difficult task—often more difficult than choosing a problem in pure science. These good applied problems are often more challenging intellectually than pure science problems.[1]

This is not to say that there should be no pure science research, but that it should be kept in proportion. Even in advanced countries basic research accounts for only about 10

[1] Lord Blackett, op. cit., II, p. 24.

per cent of the total R and D effort. In many fields the sophistication and scale of investigation involved in first-rate research have so increased that they are quite beyond the resources of individual universities, even of individual states. There is no point in indulging in second-rate research, which is merely wasteful and demoralizing.[1] In LDCs it would seem more appropriate to concentrate on the application of fundamental knowledge to local problems. University research should start in fields close to possibilities of application or to accessible local resources—fundamental problems of general interest will soon emerge.

Most universities in developing countries are completely dependent on government financial support. Unless a university contributes fully and directly to the life of its community, it cannot develop the mutual relations necessary on which to build its case for economic well-being and some degree of academic freedom.[2] In the words of the President of Tanzania, 'What we expect from our university is both a complete objectivity in the search for truth, and also commitment to our society—a desire to serve it. We expect the two things equally. And I do not believe this dual responsibility—to objectivity and to service—is impossible of fulfilment.'[3]

NEW TECHNOLOGY IN EDUCATION

If LDCs are to meet their educational requirements, extensive use is likely to be required of modern mass communications techniques applied to education, particularly through the media of television and radio. These techniques can allow good teaching to be shared widely and can help to extend the range of training opportunities, but the evidence suggests that they need to be treated with caution.

Capital costs are high, especially for television, and sound organizational, planning, and training arrangements, with the backing of an adequate technical base, are essential pre-

[1] C. F. Powell: 'Priorities in Science and Technology for Developing Countries'. In *Society and Science*, edited by M. Goldsmith and A. Mackay, Simon & Schuster, New York, 1964.

[2] A. B. Zahlan: 'Problems of Educational Manpower and Institutional Development'. In *Science and Technology in Developing Countries*, edited by C. Nader and A. B. Zahlan, C.U.P., 1969, p. 314.

[3] J. K. Nyerere: *Freedom and Socialism*. O.U.P., London, 1968, p. 182.

requisites to effective use. Given a large enough scale of operations, however, unit costs can be reasonable, as illustrated for example in Thailand, where radio instruction received by an audience of 800,000 students was estimated to cost less than 1 ct. per student hour, and in Colombia where primary training by television with an audience of 400,000 was estimated at 5 ct. per student hour.[1] In the U.K., the 'Open University', based on television courses, is due to start in 1971, and it has been estimated that, given 25,000 students each year, costs will be some 10 per cent of those in traditional universities. One of the major experiments in this field is being carried out in the Ivory Coast, where television is being extensively applied in primary, post-primary and adult education.

THE SCIENTIFIC COMMUNITY

In terms of specialized personnel, LDCs face two major problems—firstly their training in sufficient numbers and secondly ensuring their efficient use. The importance of training is well recognized, but deployment is often given far less attention. In many countries the lack of skills is aggravated by a loss of trained people through emigration, but the inefficient use of available people can entail more waste than the brain drain. As concluded in the Report of the United Nations Seminar on the Employment, Development and Role of Scientists and Technical Personnel in the Public Service of Developing Countries held at Tashkent in October 1969, 'It is the consensus that dominant emphasis must be placed on improvement of the total national environment for scientific and technical personnel to ensure not only their effective performance but also their retention in the country.'[2]

To maintain access to scientific work carried out in other countries, scientists in LDCs need to form part of the international science community. Though the published scientific paper remains an important means of communication, in many fields it no longer adequately meets the needs, and much

[1] Council on Higher Education in the American Republics: *Educational Technology and the University*. New York, 1969.
[2] U.N.: Preliminary Report on the United Nations Inter-regional Seminar on Employment, Development and Role of Scientists and Technical Personnel in the Public Service of Developing Countries, Tashkent, October 1969, p. 23.

communication depends on informal contacts between scientists. Scientific conferences and meetings provide a forum for both the formal communication process of presenting papers and informal conversations, but often the latest research results are exchanged orally at these meetings and are only printed much later. Many LDCs have problems because of a lack of personal contact with international science. Fostering these contacts can also help to relieve the sense of isolation that scientists in developing countries sometimes feel because of the relatively limited range of scientific activities carried out in their own country. This is undoubtedly one of the many factors which contribute to the brain drain, and arrangements for international research co-operation might help to reduce this loss. These arrangements could follow the prototype of the International Centre for Theoretical Physics at Trieste, which reserves 50 per cent of its posts for scientists from LDCs, provided they devote the greater part of their activities to research in their own countries, or the proposed International Centre of Insect Physiology and Ecology at Nairobi, which was mentioned in an earlier chapter (p. 92).

But there is a danger in too much involvement in international science. Given the tendency to concentrate on pure science, scientists in LDCs can sometimes become more concerned with forming part of an international intellectual *élite* than with helping to solve local practical problems. Governments and scientific communities need to work together to identify the role which scientists can play in development, and to ensure their active participation. Scientists and technical personnel must be involved in national policy development. To this end the Tashkent Seminar suggested that

within the framework of national science and technology a special need exists for Governments to direct the minds of scientists and engineers to increased identification of those scientific and technological areas with great potential for contributing to national development and national economic independence. As a general policy they should not be limited to operating within the field of their own specialised training, but should also be encouraged to give critical and constructive suggestions on administrative, technical and other problems.[1]

[1] Ibid., p. 5.

There is a strong need to build up the relationship and the communications between the science community and the policy-making component of government. But the involvement of scientists in policy-making and planning should not be restricted to a small number of the most senior research workers or academics. Scientific and technical personnel should be encouraged to establish and expand scientific, technical, and other professional societies to allow a broader range of participation.

National science policies should include consideration of working conditions, career, status, and prestige of scientists and technologists, who must themselves be involved in the formulation and implementation of such policies. The personal motivations of scientists and technologists are of course very varied. Prestige, intellectual curiosity, the social utility, or scientific significance of their work, all may play a part, but due attention has also to be given to adequate incentives and rewards. In most LDCs, a substantial proportion of scientific and technical personnel will be employed in government service. Traditional civil service systems may need to be modified to attract, develop, and retain the quality and numbers of highly trained specialists required. Many government research organizations have met serious recruitment problems, partly because of a lack of incentives. To help overcome such problems research organizations have often been granted an autonomous status independent of civil service regulations, such as, for example, the Applied Scientific Research Corporation of Thailand.

Most scientific research workers experience a loss of creativity as they approach middle age. A minority do not, and can continue to serve usefully as research leaders and directors, but save for these few a permanent research career should not be encouraged. To keep a laboratory scientifically alive a continuous flow of fresh talent is needed. The career structure should therefore allow research workers to progress into other fields, in production, administration, or teaching, as they grow older, so as to gain the full benefits of their experience. The effective economic exploitation of science and technology requires strong inter-connecting links between universities, research centres, and the production system, including agriculture as well as industry. One mechanism which helps linkage is the mobility of scientific and technical personnel between the different sectors. There may be administrative obstacles to this mobility, such as salary structure and non-transferable pension rights, but closer attention may also be needed to career planning and in-service training.

The brain drain has been mentioned at several points in this book. Numerous studies of the various aspects of this problem have been undertaken, so that even a summary analysis of their findings is not possible here. But what does seem clear is that any alleviation will require initiatives in both developed and developing countries.[1] Undoubtedly the strengthening and improved effectiveness of the scientific and technological base in any LDC will be a major factor in countering the temptations of the developed world.

MANAGERS AND ENTREPRENEURS

The direct responsibility for the effective operation and use of any nation's material and human resources falls largely on its managers—in industry, agriculture, or commerce, whether under private or public ownership. Civil servants in the public sector of LDCs often have a more direct managerial responsibility than in most developed market economies, particularly in the planning of industrialization programmes, the management of public enterprises, and in marketing and industrial relations. Managers have a vital strategic role to play in economic development and in raising a country's standard of living. The proper application of scientific management may have more far-reaching effects than the application of the natural sciences. Yet it has been claimed that 'one of the major bars to rapid economic and social development is the failure of too many key leaders (in developing countries) to give more than lip service to modern management practices'.[2] For a wide range of social, cultural, and other reasons, there is often little appreciation of the decisive importance of management.

[1] A. Parthasarathi: 'Some suggestions for national and international action to combat the flight of talent from developing countries'. *Proceedings of the Nineteenth Pugwash Conference on Science and World Affairs*, held at Sochi, U.S.S.R., October 1969.

[2] Proceedings of a World Conference on International Transfer of Management Skills, Turin, Italy, November 1969, p. 30.

If development plans are to succeed, however, a prime objective in LDCs should be the motivation and training of managers to create and build modern economic enterprises. Management training is usually more urgent than technical training, and is required at all levels—top, middle, technician, and supervisory. Practical experience is a necessary component of management training, but should be backed by formal courses and on-the-job follow-up. But while training and consultancy programmes at the enterprise level can widen the range of techniques at management's disposal, their use depends also on environmental factors.

A survey of management problems in LDCs carried out by the United Nations Research Institute for Social Development[1] gave the following results:

1. The management system found in both public and private enterprises was very often characterized by problems associated with a high degree of centralization of authority in the office of the top management and lack of delegation which created difficulties in the way of adoption of modern management methods. The principle reasons for this lack of delegation of authority were transfer to the enterprise of the traditional authority system, patriarchal roles, respect for age and superiors; lack of confidence of the top managers in the competence of their subordinates; lack of trust in subordinates and suspiciousness of outsiders.

2. A second and related major problem was the fact that managerial decisions were often made without adequate consultations with subordinates and without sufficient flow of information from relevant departments within the firm.

3. A third problem centred in achievement orientation. Both in public and private firms, there was reported to be a concern for achievement on the part of managerial personnel, but for individual achievement rather than company achievement. Incentives like personal remuneration, job security, and

[1] Research Notes, United Nations Research Institute for Social Development, No. 2, Geneva, July 1969, p. 51.

personal prestige carried more weight than incentives to build up a solidly established company. Orientation towards innovation and risk-taking was relatively weak, with a strong emphasis on planning for short-term profitability.

4. The application of modern techniques is sometimes highly dependent on factors outside the enterprise, as in the application of marketing research and marketing organization. The introduction of long-range planning met with the greatest difficulties. Strong obstacles were also found in the introduction of systematic decentralization and plant communications.

The socio-cultural constraints on management attitudes merit more searching attention. There may be a need to adjust management techniques to suit the circumstances, probably not so much in techniques such as production management and cost accounting, but where socio-cultural factors and traditions are more significant, as in personnel relations or marketing, extensive re-thinking may be required. Long-term action to meet management needs should be backed by systematic research on the management process, managerial behaviour, and training methods. Management education is still not considered respectable in some circles, but links need to be developed between management training and the higher education system.

Little attention has been paid in most countries to the need to develop entrepreneurs capable of setting up new enterprises. An entrepreneurial spirit is probably an innate gift, but it is now becoming generally recognized that various training methods and measures directed towards the individual and towards the environment can encourage and strengthen latent abilities. The basic factor seems to be motivation, and training programmes should be founded on research in achievement motivation.[1] According to McClelland, for example, the main hindrance to the emergence of an entrepreneur is the weakness of his motive to become one. Tests in India with his training methods applied to businessmen selected as potential entrepreneurs have met

[1] ILO: 'Inter-regional Technical Meeting cum Study Tour on Management of Small Enterprises', Turin, Italy, October 1968, p. 9.

with some success,[1] and further trials are being carried out in Africa, in association with the International Labour Office. But the successful development of a domestic entrepreneurial class cannot be expected in a hostile environment, and without supporting services—technical as well as financial.

[1] D. C. McClelland and D. G. Winter: *Motivating Economic Achievement*. The Free Press, New York, 1969.

Summary

The theme of this book has been the application of science and technology as an instrument for economic growth. This is not to denigrate the other great values of science, nor to worship at the shrine of the GNP. But the alleviation of poverty in LDCs is of dominant importance, and requires economic growth as well as social justice. It is all very well for people in advanced countries to speak about the 'dethronement of the GNP', but in poorer countries a considerable increase in GNP is bound to remain a major target in development, though with due regard to the social and environmental consequences, and to the importance of a more equitable distribution of wealth and of increased employment. Economic growth is desirable not as an end in itself, but as a means to other ends.

In any attempt at a balanced and detailed discussion of a complex subject there is always the danger of losing the principal emphases. The objective of this summary is to recapitulate some of the main lines of argument, so as to draw them together into a more coherent whole.

INDUSTRY AND AGRICULTURE

Economic growth requires the *concurrent development of agriculture and industry*, though in some countries minerals can also make a decisive contribution. There is a symbiotic relationship between industry and agriculture, and both must be developed together.

Associated with the rapid increase in population, *unemployment* is becoming one of the major problems of LDCs. Industrial growth is limited by many factors, and in the short term this sector cannot be expected to provide adequate employment. The numerical predominance of the non-urban population emphasizes the importance of rural development if this problem is to be solved.

INNOVATION AND INVESTMENT

The economic growth of industrialized countries has depended to a considerable extent on *technological innovation*, backed by capital investment. Innovations may range from the spectacular creation of new science-based industries, through improvements to existing products and processes, to modest but numerous gains in productivity.

In LDCs innovation has played a much smaller role. *Capital investment*, largely embodying imported technology, has been the main source of economic development.

New investment is evidently very important for continued growth, and is often essential for technological change. But in both agriculture and industry, the *improvement and adaptation* of indigenous or imported technology and *increased efficiency* in the use of resources also deserve close attention. Productivity improvements are a necessary part of the process of economic growth and stem essentially from the exploitation of improved technology.

R AND D

In an effort to engender improved technology most LDCs are striving to increase their expenditure on R and D, but it is important to recognize that R and D is but the first stage in a *continuous innovative chain* linking scientific research, market research, development design, first production, and market acceptance.

Experience elsewhere has indicated the need to keep basic and applied research in proportion to development and design, and to other scientific and technological activities. By themselves, neither the availability of scientific research facilities nor opportunities for industrial or agricultural improvement is enough to ensure economic progress. What is required is a proper *co-ordination of science, technology, and production*.

SCIENCE PLANNING

In developed countries, innovations are prompted by market pressures for lower costs, better processes or newer products, or by nationally planned efforts to meet clearly defined objectives.

In LDCs market mechanisms are inadequate, and innovation depends more on government intervention in *planning and research*.

Hence the greater importance in LDCs of national science planning at the highest political level, with supporting organizations to provide technical information and advice and to implement decisions. This implies not just a policy for scientific research, but covers the entire field of developing and making best use of the *national scientific and technological potential*, in a two-way interaction with economic and social planning. More research may be less important than strengthening the supporting service activities, and raising the general level of productive competence.

TECHNOLOGICAL COMPETENCE

No country has the capacity to meet its scientific and technological requirements from its own resources, nor would it be sound strategy to attempt to do so. For an LDC, while the local scientific and technical infrastructure is being developed, the rational emphasis will be on making the *best use of imported technology*. This requires attention both to the mechanisms for the transfer of technology, and to the level of technological competence within the productive sectors and their supporting services.

The capacity to absorb improved technology depends on the general level of skills, a *balanced distribution of scientific and technological personnel*, and an adequate supply of managerial and entrepreneurial talent. Technically-minded entrepreneurs, cost-conscious managers, innovative designers and engineers are likely to be at least as valuable as research scientists in the earlier stages of development.

In the creative and efficient use of resources—including trained personnel—*management is probably the most important factor*. In most LDCs there seems an urgent need for recognition to be given to their *decisive role*, and more attention to building up the supply of managers who are able to create and develop modern enterprises, whether in the private or the public sector.

As development proceeds, the aim will be to increase technological competence, so as to lessen technological dependence.

This involves building up a network of applied research, development, and design centres, with extension and supporting services, the effectiveness of which to a large extent depends on *good communications* within the network and externally with the productive sectors and government planning.

RESEARCH ORGANIZATION

The more basic the research the more central it can afford to be, though good communications are still vital, on the one side with international science, and on the other side with applied problems. But further along the line, as at the experimental farm or design workshop stage, the closer to production the better. *Linkages between government, production, and research are vitally important,* and their effectiveness may be more decisive than the actual physical form of the overall organization.

Modernizing agriculture requires the development of technological improvements which have been tailored to suit the particular ecological circumstances and the local farming system, which are then proved and demonstrated as worthwhile for the individual farmer, and which finally are actively 'sold' to him, in conjunction with corresponding attention to any other factors which may hinder acceptance.

Similarly, to further *industrial growth,* a research organization needs to do much more than research, it must itself take on an entrepreneurial function and carry an innovation further towards economic exploitation than is normally necessary in industrialized countries. Supporting institutions will be required to help select the most appropriate technology and to adapt it to suit local needs and conditions. As an industry develops, it is likely to meet these short-term needs increasingly through its own efforts, as through an expansion of quality control laboratories, so that the national research centres can concentrate more on longer-term problems.

CHOICE OF TECHNOLOGY

The best use of resources in LDCs requires the development of both *efficient capital-saving and efficient labour-intensive techniques.* This is essential if capital is to be used more effectively, and if the labour force is to be given useful employment.

12

While there may be limitations to adaptation and development in certain industries, there is undoubted scope to *broaden the technological spectrum* and increase the area of choice. This choice is generally made at the enterprise level, but inducements can be used to encourage decisions in any particular direction—what that direction should be is the responsibility of the government.

EDUCATION AND MANPOWER

Development and social change cannot take place without a certain minimum of scientific culture. Hence the importance of introducing *science education as early as possible*, at primary level, taking full advantage of the new approaches, including the application of advanced technologies, which have been developed in recent years, though adapting them to suit local circumstances and needs.

The specific skills required for economic development points to an increased emphasis on a wider range of secondary and post-secondary level training which is essentially vocational, though built on a sound general base. Even at university level, comparatively few narrow specialists will be required, and the major need is a *broad scientific and technological training, including related social studies*, which aims at technical competence in a wide setting. If university graduates are to get jobs, they must be educated in fields relevant to the likely employment opportunities.

Factors affecting the *productivity of expensively trained scientists and technologists*, and their preferences for fields of work, are worth examining. Status, both social and scientific, may be important, as also are incentives and rewards. The mobility of technical personnel can be an important aspect of linking research and production, and making best use of the talent available. Adequate backing support is another requirement for maximum effectiveness, particularly in the form of technicians and technical services.

DEVELOPMENT ASSISTANCE

While the economic development of LDCs has primarily to be the responsibility of these countries themselves, the rest of the world should and must help. Various proposals have been made advocating increased R and D attention in developed countries to LDC problems, but much more thought needs to be given to the mechanisms which would be required to ensure that any such efforts are not dissipated, but yield economic results. Bilateral links, co-operative research arrangements and other approaches can be useful, but the arguments advanced in this book suggest that without careful selection, together with matching attention to other limiting factors, a massive increase in research spending may be ill-advised. *Aid and trade may be more helpful than research.*

Index of Authors and Works Quoted in the Text

KRANZBURG, M. and PURSELL, C. W.: Technology in Western Civilisation. 114

LEWIS, W. A.: Development planning. 58
— The Development Process. 53, 99, 135

LITTLE, A. D.: Space technology transfer and developing nations. 107

McCLELLAND, D. C. and WINTER, D. G.: Motivating Economic Achievement. 155

MORSE, D.: Dimensions of the employment problem in developing countries. 127

MOSEMAN, A. H.: Building agricultural research systems in the developing nations. 68, 92, 93

MOSHER, A. T.: Getting agriculture moving. Essentials for development and modernisation. 59

MITCHELL, C. and SCHATAN, J.: The outlook for agricultural development in Latin America. 57, 58, 59, 77, 87

NADER, C. and ZAHLAN, A. B. (eds.): Science and Technology in Developing Countries. 148

NAYUDAMMA, Y.: Promoting the industrial application of research in an under-developed country. 27, 119, 121, 125

NOVE, A. and NEWTH, J. A.: The Soviet Middle East. 145

NYERERE, J. K.: Freedom and Socialism. 148

OECD: Conference on policies for educational growth—Conclusions. 136
— Government and technical innovation. 21
— Problems of Human Resources Planning in Latin America and in the Mediterranean Regional Project Countries. 133, 134, 139
— Reviews of national science policy—Japan. 39
— Science policy in the U.S.S.R. 46, 120

OLCESE, O.: Latin America: University education in agriculture. 142

OLDHAM, C. D. G., FREEMAN, C., and TURKCAN, E.: Transfer of technology to developing countries. 13

PARTHASARATHI, A.: Some suggestions for national and international action to combat the flight of talent from developing countries. 152
— Universities and Nation Building. 146

PARTHASARATHI, G.: Education and Social Progress. 135, 142

PARKER, PETER: The Times. 109

General Index

Afghanistan, 54
Africa: agricultural development, 18; agricultural research, 68–9, 91, 93; education, 136; food imports, 85; industry/agriculture interdependence, 88; rural population, 60; research centres, 52, 91–2
Agriculture: co-operatives, 86; credit, 59, 75, 82, 86; crop diversification, 63, 83; pests and diseases, 18, 64, 84, 92; economic growth and, 17, 57–8, 97; employment in, 17, 60, 63, 79–80, 136; exports, 17–18, 56–7, 83–4, 98; extension services, 18, 45, 71–8; farmers' incomes, 85–6; interdependence with industry, 17, 56–8, 84, 88, 97–8, 130; manpower, 89–90, 136, 142, 144; marketing problems, 82–4; mechanization, 61–2, 79–80, 130; multiple cropping, 62, 80–2; population growth and, 17, 55–6, 60; post-harvest losses, 82–3; production incentives, 18, 59, 71–2, 74–5, 83, 88–9; storage problems, 82–3; technical assistance, 89–90; technology improvement, 15, 63–6, 159; tools, improved, 129–30; yield, 79, 80–1
Agricultural development: 16–19, 53–59; capital intensive, 60–2, 88; Japanese model, 60–1, 88; labour intensive, 63, 88; limiting factors, 18, 59, 63–5, 71–2, 76, 86–9; Mexican model, 60, 61; objectives, 59–60; political costs, 89; resistance to change in, 72–3; strategy, 59–63, 89
Agricultural innovations: acceptability of, 71, 73–4; divisibility, 74; feasibility, 65, 67, 71, 74, 78, 82–9; reversibility, 74; risks to farmers, 72, 74; sequence, 73, 86; small farmers and, 75
Agricultural research: 19, 43, 65–71, 90–3, 133; co-operation, 52, 90–3; on cropping systems, 82; expenditure on, 69–71; organization, 66–9; and

private enterprise, 70–1; **profit-ability**, 70
Ahmadu Bello University (Nigeria), 33, 76
Algeria, 115
Argentina, 41, 58
Australia, 109

Battelle Memorial Institute, 31, 115
Bell Laboratories, 106
BIRPI (United International Bureaux for the Protection of Intellectual Property), 114
Bolivia, 146
Brain drain, 28, 147, 149–50, 152
Brazil, 22, 99, 100, 107
Business technology, transfer of, 110

Canada, 21, 30
Capital substitutes, 129
Cereals: Africa—imports, 85; new varieties, 17–18, 53–6, 80–1, 85–6; production costs, 63, 83; storage, 82–83; yield improvement, 54–5
Ceylon, rice production, 55
Change: social, 57, 72–3; technical, 21, 72–3
Chile, 58, 84
China, 22, 130–1
CIAT, *see* International Centre for Tropical Agriculture
CIMMYT, *see* International Maize and Wheat Improvement Centre
Cocoa, 65, 84, 93
Colombia, 77, 91, 149
Consultants, 115–16, 147
Co-production schemes, 111
COSTED (Committee on Science & Technology), viii, xv
Cost effectiveness analysis, 136–7
Cotton Research Corporation, 90
CSIR (Council for Scientific & Industrial Research, India), 117

Dairy produce, 85

Design capability, transfer, 111
Development: agricultural, *see* Agricultural development; and agricultural/industrial interdependence, 17, 56–8, 84, 88, 97–8, 130, 156; assistance, 5, 30, 160–1; definition, 4; industrial *see* Industrialization; and science policy, 7, 16, 36, 41, 104; rural, 133, 135, 140–1, 156; universities' role in, 31–3, 141–8
Documentation centres, 15

Earth sciences, 43, 144
Ecology and agricultural technology, 6, 15, 18, 64
Economic growth: and agriculture, 18, 57, 97; and education, 134, 136; and health, xi; in industrialized countries, 7; and innovation, 8, 10, 45, 102–5; and international corporations, 20, 109–11; and science policy, 15, 34, 37, 51, 104; and technical progress, 5–7, 102–3; and technology imports, 12, 48, 100, 111–14, 116
Education: adapted to local needs, 31, 141–2; and economic growth, 134, 136; expenditure, 132–3, 136–7; graduate numbers, 142–4; higher, 31–3, 141–8, 160; and manpower, 133–7, 160; post-graduate, 49, 147; research, 139; rural, 136, 140–1; science, 137–9, 142–4, 146; secondary, 135, 139–40, 160; teachers training colleges, 139; technical, 135–6, 140–3, 147; television and radio in, 148–9; vocational, 135–6, 139–41, 160
Employment: and agriculture, 17, 60, 62–3, 79–80, 130, 136; capital costs of, 25; and choice of technology, 25, 126–31; and vocational training, 141
Engineering: design as substitute for capital, 129; research expenditure, 9, 45, 117
Engineers, numbers in LDCs, 142–3
Entrepreneurs, training of, 154–5
Environmental studies, 16, 43, 51, 64, 95
Exports: agricultural, 17–18, 56–7, 83–84, 98; manufactured, 20, 24, 100, 123

Family Planning, xi

Farmers: associations, 78; small-scale, 17, 63, 75, 88
Fertilizers, 17, 54, 64, 89, 97, 128
Fiat Motor Company, 111
Fishing, development of, 19, 93, 95
Food production: and population growth, 53, 55–6, 83; and storage, 82
Ford Foundation, 30, 52, 67, 90–1
Ford Motor Company, 130
Forestry, 19, 93–5
France, 12–13, 67, 90

GDP, *see* Gross Domestic Product
General Motors, 109
Germany: East, 9; West, 10–13
Ghana, 77–8, 84
GNP, *see* Gross National Product
Green revolution, 18, 53–6, 83
Gross Domestic Product, 1
Gross National Product, xii, xiii, 1–3, 156

Health standards, xi

ICIPE, *see* International Centre for Insect Physiology & Ecology
ICSU, *see* International Council of Scientific Unions
IITA, *see* International Institute of Tropical Agriculture
Imperial Chemical Industries Ltd., 29, 110
Import substitution, 20, 98–100
India: car component exports, 130; cereal production, 53–5, 83; education, 133–4; industrial research, 117; land reform, 88; management training, 110; political costs of agrarian modernization, 89; process plant industry, 101; rural labour shortage, 62
Industrialization: choice of technology, 25, 126–31; consultants, 115–16, 147; and economic development, 19–21, 96; import substitution, 20, 98–100; management, 7, 15, 102, 104, 152–5, 158; research, 20–1, 96, 100, 116–26; support services, 98, 103, 105, 122–4; transfer of technology, 20, 23, 107–9, 112–16
Industrial services, international sale of, 111